11/06

11/06

Managing Library Volunteers

A Practical Toolkit

PRESTON DRIGGERS
EILEEN DUMAS

AMERICAN LIBRARY ASSOCIATION
Chicago and London
2002

Composition by ALA Editions in New Baskerville and Optima using QuarkXPress 4.1 on a PC platform

Printed on 50-pound white offset, a pH-neutral stock, and bound in 10-point cover stock by Data Reproductions

The paper used in this publication meets the minimum requirements of American National Standard for Information Sciences—Permanence of Paper for Printed Library Materials, ANSI Z39.48-1992. ∞

ISBN: 0-8389-0806-3

Printed in the United States of America

06 05 04 03 02   5 4 3 2 1

CONTENTS

PART III ■ TRAINING AND DEVELOPMENT

PART IV ■ AWARDS AND RECOGNITION

PART V ■ VOLUNTEER RULES AND DISCIPLINE

PART VI ■ VOLUNTEER RECORD KEEPING

FIGURE AND SAMPLES

ACKNOWLEDGMENTS

This manual dates back to the fall of 1991 when Eileen Dumas of the Aurora Public Library and Terry Nelson of the Denver Public Library recognized a need to form a group of library staff who coordinated and managed volunteer programs. Among others, Dumas and Nelson felt that there was a lack of information available that directly addressed the unique role of library volunteer managers.

A new group was organized in 1992, called "Metro Area Library Volunteer Coordinators Council." The group expanded over time to include representation from all the major libraries along the Colorado Front Range. (For a history of the group, see Catherine Childs and John Waite Bowers, "Introducing the Colorado Libraries Volunteer Managers Council," *Colorado Libraries* 23 (summer 1997): 36–39.)

During the second year of the group's existence, Preston Driggers of the Douglas Public Library District became a member, adding his knowledge of human resources and risk management to the group. As information accumulated on volunteer program activities, group members suggested that a manual be written based on their experiences. The idea seemed a natural extension of the group meetings and two authors agreed to take on the task. . . . However, the early drafts of this manual were not circulated until the summer of 1996. Both authors are grateful to the members of the now renamed, "Colorado Volunteer Managers Council," for their open discussions on the finer points of managing successful programs. Without their contribution, this manual would not have been as complete.

Special acknowledgments are due (in alphabetical order) to Willo Auger, Darrell Chayne, Catherine Childs, Belinda Goelbel, Ann Keller, Mary Lou McNatt, C. Terry Nelson, Liesel Schmid, Ed Stephen, Ann Tomas, and Midge Trueman. We would also like to extend our appreciation to the volunteer managers who were part of our group in the past and have gone on to new positions. They too are contributors.

Although many individuals from large and small programs have contributed, the authors accept responsibility for any errors, omissions, or confusion that the reader may encounter.

Finally, as one volunteer manager stated, "I have the best of all jobs because I work with library volunteers. These are wonderful people." We hope that is your experience too.

We wish to offer special acknowledgment to the following libraries for the use of their materials as reproducible samples:

Adams Public Library
Arapahoe Public Library
Aurora Public Library
Boulder Public Library
Denver Public Library
Douglas Public Library District

Englewood Public Library
Fort Collins Public Library
Jefferson Public Library
Mesa County Public Library
Pikes Peak Library District

HOW TO USE THIS MANUAL

This manual is designed for multiple uses. For a library staff member suddenly placed in the role of volunteer manager, this manual is a ready guide with reproducible samples, policies, and practical discussions on establishing a new volunteer program. Topical sections allow quick access to those problems that must be addressed immediately. Each section covers options for small, medium, and large libraries.

For a staff member taking over an existing volunteer program, the discussion points serve as ready reference for explaining the underlying basis for existing procedures. Individuals trained in library and information science are often unfamiliar with the human resource, legal, and risk management requirements in operating a successful volunteer program. This manual provides information on these topics.

For the experienced volunteer manager, the manual can be disassembled and put into a three-ring binder. The sections can then be expanded with current articles, information on volunteer management from the Internet, or sample volunteer forms, recognition awards, and policies used by other libraries. This approach allows the manual to become a customized resource for a particular library volunteer program.

Setting up or operating a volunteer program is a challenge. The overriding goal of this manual is to help you, the volunteer manager, meet the challenge.

TERMINOLOGY

As an auxiliary duty to their regular library jobs, staff members usually coordinate library volunteers. Very few libraries enjoy the luxury of having a paid staff member whose sole function is to manage a volunteer program. When a staff member shifts hats and works with the volunteer program, she may be known as volunteer coordinator, supervisor, manager, administrator, or director of volunteer services. Titles and range of duties vary, but for consistency this book uses the term "volunteer manager" to represent staff who are assigned the responsibility of managing a volunteer program.

There is an ongoing controversy within the professional library community about whether to use the term *customer* or *patron* when referring to a library user. There are good arguments for either word. For consistency, the authors have chosen to use the term "customer" without suggesting any commitment for or against this particular terminology.

INTRODUCTION
The Volunteer Program Cycle

The Volunteer Program Cycle demonstrates how all the parts of a volunteer program are interrelated (see figure 1). Recruitment is successful when library needs are assessed and job descriptions are written based on those needs. The placement of a volunteer can happen only after the volunteer manager has matched her skills and interests to the library's needs, thus beginning the volunteer's transition from "outsider" to "insider" as a member of the library's human resources.

The number of volunteer positions at any one time is based on the staff's perceptions of volunteers. When staff are favorably impressed by the work accomplished by volunteers, the number of individuals who are willing to supervise or work with them increases. With more staff involvement, the number of volunteer positions or task slots that become open grows. The growth of volunteer positions is, in turn, influenced by the volunteers' task performance; the better the volunteers perform, the more likely the staff are to hire additional volunteers. And volunteer performance is positively correlated to selecting, matching, and training new volunteers.

FIGURE 1
Enhancing Library Services: The Volunteer Program Cycle

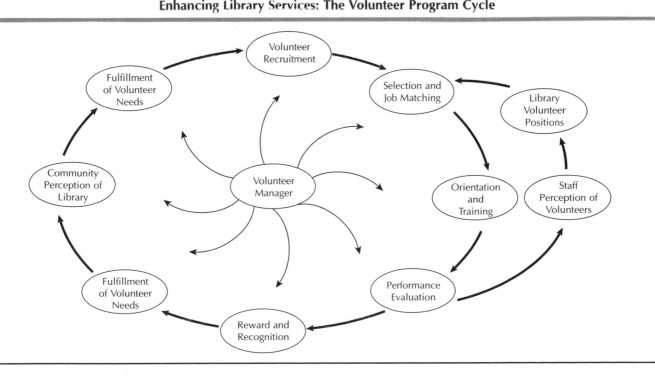

Reward, recognition, and a verbal or written thank you for a job well done enhance the volunteer's sense of fulfillment. When people are pleased with their library experience, they will generally share these feelings with others, thereby encouraging positive community perceptions of the library. In turn, positive community perceptions may increase the number of individuals who want to become library volunteers. The program cycle continues ad infinitum.

In the day-to-day operation of the library, the role of volunteer manager is to find ways that volunteers can enhance library services. When the role of volunteer manager is externally focused, the position becomes an integral part of library community relations. This manual is a practical guide to assist you in using the Volunteer Program Cycle to make your program a success.

SECTION

1

The Value of Volunteerism

The value associated with volunteerism goes to the heart of our democratic society and the history of community libraries. In some instances, paid staff owe their library careers to the field of volunteerism. In many small towns today, public libraries remain open through the combined efforts of the Friends of the Library, volunteer trustees, and a small, dedicated group of community volunteers. Moreover, projects too costly to justify hiring extra staff are successfully carried out with the help of volunteers. In today's economy and most probably that of the future, the importance of volunteers cannot be dismissed as a passing fad.

In the broadest sense, library volunteerism is one way of fostering the democratic ideal of community participation. It provides individuals with an opportunity to work actively in their local government. In the narrowest sense, volunteerism is one part of the total dialog between the community and the library. This dialog is enriched as meaningful volunteer opportunities emerge.

Community participation in local libraries ensures that there will be a continuous flow of diverse ideas, skills, talents, and energies that will enable the library to continue to be a dynamic institution, a place where individuals and families choose to spend their time and give their support.

Keeping the library vital requires hard work to connect all aspects of library services to the community. Library volunteering underscores and enhances this connection.

The following are thematic value statements that can be used in whole or in part to create a set of values for your program or to incorporate into your volunteer program mission statement.

VALUE STATEMENTS

- The library defines volunteerism as a resource for both the library and the community. Library volunteering supports the greater values associated with individual choice and participation that underlie a democracy.

- Volunteerism is a vital part of the enhancing dialog and social contact between the library and the local community.

- The value of library volunteerism lies in the unique abilities and skills of each individual. When volunteers are placed in appropriate jobs, their personal contributions reflect and enhance the library's defined values as found in its mission and goal statements.

- The value of library volunteerism is to support the individual's need to be a productive and caring community member.

SECTION
2

Volunteer Program Mission Statement

Why is a mission statement important for a library volunteer program? It provides the purpose and goals, establishes a strong foundation, and offers consistent direction. A mission statement also ensures that your program is not working in isolation and in opposition to the library's purpose and goals. Therefore, the mission statement of your volunteer program needs to be included as part of the library's overall mission statement and have the support of the top administrator.

Here are four quick tips to help you write a simple mission statement:

1. Write the statement in less than 100 to 150 words, in a clear and motivational tone.
2. Define the specific aspects of the program in terms of purposes and reasons, the target volunteer populations and groups to be served, and major functions and activities.
3. Decide on the long-term goals.
4. Decide on the core values that will underlie the program.

A mission statement needs to be broad enough to encompass diverse programs, even if these programs are still in the planning stages. For example, a general program directed toward volunteers assisting with the necessary, routine support tasks could complement a future program that is focused on serving the homebound. Ideally, the mission statement will not change with additional programs.

WRITING A VOLUNTEER MISSION STATEMENT

One way to think through the process of writing a mission statement is to answer the following questions as they relate to your program:

- What is the purpose of the program?

    (*Purpose:* To attract community volunteers who want to work with the paid staff to enhance library services)

- Whom are you trying to attract to your program?

    (*General Target Group:* Community adults and youth)

- What do you want to achieve with the program?

    (*Achievement:* To provide enhanced services with volunteers and staff as equals)

- What are the benefits of the program for the library, staff, and community?

    (*Benefits:* Opportunities for citizens to make positive contributions to library operations)

Below are examples of four completed mission statements:

(1) The mission of the Library's volunteer program is to encourage and expand the involvement of community volunteers. They will work with the staff, as partners, to provide service to others by supporting, preserving, and promoting free and easy access to ideas and information.

(2) The Library will provide opportunities so that all volunteers find satisfaction in serving their community through their affiliation with this program.

(3) The library asks volunteers to give their talents and energy to supplement and complement the staff. This frees staff to initiate new and innovative programs. A benefit of a successful program can result in volunteers becoming public advocates for the library and its services.

(4) The library holds that volunteers are an important human resource. They have the right to be treated as co-workers, trained in a professional manner, and given richly deserved recognition.

3

Volunteer Program Benefits and Purposes

As the volunteer manager, you are responsible for "selling" the benefits and purposes of your program to the library staff. In the beginning, the library staff may not appreciate the benefits. Instead, they may view the program as entailing added work and hidden expenses for training, supervising, and evaluating the volunteers, and administering the program. However, if the benefits are weighed against the costs, then even the most questioning and negative employees will begin to appreciate the value of volunteers to the library. You can change negative attitudes to positive attitudes by emphasizing program benefits at staff meetings, through memos, or via internal staff newsletters.

The following three general categories are influenced by the use of volunteers:

1. Library services;
2. Personal enrichment; and
3. Community and citizenship values.

After exploring each of these areas in more detail, you will begin to understand the benefits and cost savings to your library.

LIBRARY SERVICES

Volunteers can improve library services in the following specific ways:

- Expand support for routine tasks and special library projects;
- Enhance the level and quality of customer services; and
- Provide supplemental expertise.

Expand Staff Support

How can you develop volunteer job opportunities to help staff with routine tasks or special projects? First, send out a survey or ask specific staff members what tasks or programs are not getting adequate attention and need extra help. The responses will tell you how volunteers can best be used immediately or in the near future. For example, shelf reading, shelving or mending books, or transplanting and pruning indoor plants are tasks that need to be done, but often the staff does not have time to do them or cannot do them on a regular basis. Volunteers can be assigned to work in these areas with little or no training.

Enhance the Level and Quality of Customer Service

Volunteers can be trained to teach customers how to search the World Wide Web or how to use the online catalog. This training immediately improves customer service by providing customers with individualized help. It also enables the reference staff to concentrate their efforts on customers needing assistance with research or locating specific information in the reference area. In addition to teaching computer skills, volunteers can call customers about their reserve items, work on an information desk, or assist in technical services such as deleting items from a database or bar coding and stamping new books. All of these tasks improve the level and quality of service that the library can provide.

Provide Supplemental Expertise

Volunteers bring their skills, talents, and training to the library organization. Skills and training in computer hardware and specific software programs can help a department or small library set up database files, develop specialized reporting forms, or run mail-merge programs. Retired elementary school teachers can volunteer their time to read or tell stories to young children during a morning story time or at a local day-care center. Former department store "window dressers" are excellent resources for creating library displays. Graphic artists can design flyers or posters for special programs or recruitment advertisements. The library would have to pay hundreds of dollars to hire these experts for one day or several weeks. A volunteer program gives the library an opportunity to recruit and benefit from this talent.

PERSONAL ENRICHMENT

Volunteering can provide an individual with opportunities for personal satisfaction, growth, and enrichment. Specifically, volunteers can:

- Acquire new technical, office, administrative, or customer service skills;
- Gain a sense of personal achievement from learning a new skill or successfully completing a project; and
- Develop feelings of self-worth and pride from helping others.

Volunteers are often surprised at the range of activities and skills that are required to run a library. At first, many volunteers are excited about learning a new skill, such as reading to seniors in nursing homes, presenting puppet shows for children, or preparing bibliographies, but at the same time they may be apprehensive about starting a new task and working in an unfamiliar environment. The strength of your volunteer program will lie in your ability to allay these apprehensions by ensuring that all new volunteers receive the necessary support from their immediate supervisors and adequate on-the-job training. This attention to volunteers' needs will encourage an atmosphere of success for everyone.

For young adults entering the job market for the first time, the benefits they derive from learning skills such as word processing, the operation of a high-speed copying machine, or the basics of handling angry customers while working on the job are invaluable.

Individuals who become volunteers after losing a spouse, their jobs, or being relocated from another city derive benefits from the structure of the tasks they perform and the friendship of individual library staff.

COMMUNITY AND CITIZENSHIP VALUES

A public library is intimately linked to the community through its outreach efforts. By starting a volunteer program, the library encourages a two-way dialog that supports local citizenship and community values that benefit and enhance all concerned. Specifically, these values include:

Community Values:

Create a positive image of the library in the community;

Bring information about local ideas, issues, and concerns back to the library so that staff and administration can better meet community needs; and

Demonstrate community support for the library by encouraging local citizens to become "shareholders" in a local government agency.

Citizenship Values:

Meet school requirements for community service hours;

Afford people the opportunity to make legal restitution to the community through library service; and

Meet civic, service, and religious groups' requirements for community service.

From his or her unique perspective, the individual defines the meaning of the term "citizenship values." For some local residents, being a good citizen merely means paying the mill levy or property tax. For others, it means giving something back to their community in terms of time, money, or unique expertise (this is seen in the volunteer who organizes a fund-raising effort, holds a book sale, or runs a library gift shop).

As a volunteer manager, you will learn more about how your community feels about the library than the technical services administrator, who has little public contact. At the same time, volunteers are taking information about your program and the library back to their family and friends. This exchange benefits the library as part of a positive and essential public relations effort.

BENEFIT/PURPOSE STATEMENTS

You probably will not notice all of these benefits at the beginning. What is important is that by working with the staff and administrators you will eventually develop a benefits/purpose statement for your specific volunteer program.

As you scan the sample benefit statements, note that each statement can be written as either a "purpose statement" for a specific program or as a benefit for librarians, library support staff, administrators, volunteers, customers, or members of the community at large. If someone or some group does not benefit from a program, it will probably not be successful.

Hint: Do not disregard your draft set of statements because you may find them useful in constructing your volunteer recruitment flyers or other volunteer notices.

Benefit Statements

Library Services

Our volunteers supplement, enhance, and support library staff by meeting the demands for quality public service.

Effective use of library volunteers can extend the value of every tax dollar by providing an increased pool of labor and a larger diversity of human resources.

Volunteers contribute to the success of _____ library program by providing enhanced customer service.

_____ Library's use of volunteers helps to maintain quality children's services.

Personal Enhancement

Library volunteerism empowers individuals to reach their potential as productive members of the community and to make positive contributions to the quality of community life.

Library volunteering can serve as on-the-job training.

Our library volunteers gain a sense of personal achievement by being an important part of our _____ program.

Library volunteers gain a sense of personal esteem by sharing their talents to help others through our "Reading to Seniors Program."

Community/Citizenship Values

Our volunteer program provides an opportunity for citizens to volunteer and make positive contributions to the _____ Library.

Community volunteers bring good feelings and positive attitudes to the staff by freely giving their unique talents.

Volunteering encourages individuals in the community to appreciate the _____ Library.

Volunteering encourages citizens to become familiar with the library resources and its services.

Volunteers reflect the ideas and concerns of the community and therefore bring special awareness to the library's planning and administrative processes.

_____ Library provides volunteer hours for court-assigned community restitution.

Our volunteer program provides the opportunity for youth to complete their community service academic requirements.

SECTION

4

Volunteer Administration

The objective of this section is to give you an overview of the key areas you need to consider when setting up (or taking over) the administration of a volunteer program. The following nine points will help you establish general guidelines and a philosophy:

1. The volunteer manager and the organizational chart;
2. The volunteer manager's job description;
3. The volunteer's job description;
4. Volunteer orientation and training;
5. Volunteer communication and feedback;
6. Volunteer performance evaluation and recognition;
7. Educating the library staff about volunteers;
8. Valuing volunteers; and
9. Researching volunteer information.

THE VOLUNTEER MANAGER
AND THE ORGANIZATIONAL CHART

Whether you are a full- or a part-time volunteer administrator, you need to know where you fit into the organization as a whole. Will your volunteer program have its own budget or will your funds be part of someone else's budget? Whose approval do you need to develop and expand your program? For example, do you report to a key administrator, such as the human resources manager, a branch manager, or someone else? Do you have two supervisors, one for your regular library duties and another for your volunteer duties? Are you expected to recruit and coordinate volunteers for your library alone or are you expected to manage all the volunteers for the entire library system? When you have clear answers to these questions, you and the other staff members will understand how the volunteer program operates within the library system.

As a rule, the more departments your volunteer program includes (for example, circulation, reference, children's services, administration, and so forth), the higher up in the administrative hierarchy you should report if the program is to succeed. For example, if you are asked to work with volunteers across library departments, but you report to a department manager, it is unlikely that the other managers will accept your administrative efforts. Regardless of how professionally you behave, these managers are apt to perceive your coordination efforts as "interfering" in their respective departments. In such a situation, you may reach a high level of frustration because you do not have the authority to coordinate volunteers across multiple departments or branches.

On the other hand, if you work with volunteers in a small branch library and report directly to the branch manager, you will be more likely to have the support of the other staff because you have the authority to use volunteers across a wide range of branch services.

Similarly, in a large library system, if you are the volunteer manager for the children's department and report directly to the supervisor of children and youth services, you will probably find your work environment very satisfying.

It is always important to work with your supervisor to define your position within your particular library system.

THE VOLUNTEER MANAGER'S JOB DESCRIPTION

Initially, you probably did not have a written job description, especially if you were the first person assigned to manage the volunteer program. It is important to make sure you have a written job description at the outset to clarify your duties and explain how you will be evaluated or how you will evaluate your own performance.

A job description for a library volunteer coordinator is shown in sample 4-1. You can use this sample as a starting point to help you customize a job description for your specific position requirements.

Clearly defined job expectations and job descriptions can reduce potential difficulties with management and staff. For example, if one of your duties is to visit local groups to recruit volunteers, does this mean "on your own time" without pay? Or are you expected to visit only groups that are available during your normal working hours? Can you juggle your hours so that you are able to visit the groups whenever they meet? If you are performing two functions (reference librarian and volunteer manager), do you have some leeway to shift or trade hours to administer the program?

THE VOLUNTEER'S JOB DESCRIPTION

Volunteers want to be successful. A key to helping volunteers succeed is ensuring that they know at the outset what is expected of them. That is why a job description is important.

You can share written job descriptions with new volunteers during their initial interview so that they can decide which job is the best "fit" for their interests and skills. In addition, by going over this information in the beginning, you indirectly let applicants know that these jobs include expectations for successful performance.

It is important that you prepare volunteer job descriptions, even if they are written sets of task procedures, because with written job descriptions, both you and the volunteer will have fewer problems over the long term.

DOUGLAS PUBLIC LIBRARY
Position Description
VOLUNTEER SERVICES COORDINATOR

GENERAL STATEMENT OF DUTIES: The incumbent develops, administers, and coordinates the effective District-wide recruitment and use of volunteer talents as a community resource that supplements and complements those of the staff.

FUNCTIONAL RESPONSIBILITY: Responsible on a daily basis for the implementation and administration of the Library District Volunteer Services Program.

EXAMPLES OF DUTIES
(The following are intended to be illustrative only and not all-inclusive)

Essential Functions

Plans and coordinates with library staff input, the effective use of volunteer talent and services for District branches, departments, functions, and programs. Assesses volunteer staffing requirements and makes recommendations on volunteer staffing needs, new volunteer programs, or improvements in existing programs to the Personnel Manager.

Actively recruits volunteers for all library branches, departments, and programs. Designs recruitment materials, recruitment strategies and coordinates with staff and volunteers in the planning and implementing of recruitment activities.

Works closely with staff to develop volunteer job descriptions and appropriate branch volunteer tasks assignments. Determines current and future needs for volunteers through staff interviews, Library Friends groups, Library Foundation staff and members, and patron surveys.

Develops the District Volunteer Mission Statement, Policy and Procedural Manual, volunteer rules, staff supervision guidelines, and the Volunteer Handbook. Stays informed on new volunteer approaches, legislative, legal, and risk-management issues in the use of volunteers.

Conducts training workshops for staff members supervising volunteers and in their use of effective volunteer management principles.

Reviews prospective volunteer application forms, conducts initial volunteer interviews, reference checks, background or driver's license reviews, and makes recommendations for placement. Provides new volunteers with preliminary library orientation.

Assesses volunteer-staff relationships, volunteer performance and satisfaction levels. Addresses requests for volunteer reassignments, problem solving, and terminations.

Designs appropriate volunteer awards, recognition, and benefit programs.

Establishes communications through a newsletter, bulletin boards, e-mail, newspaper articles, and other media with volunteers, staff, Library Friends, patrons, and the community about volunteer Library activities and programs. Advertises a calendar of volunteer events and publicizes volunteer accomplishments.

Establishes regular outreach efforts and serves as a liaison with local volunteer organizations and agencies. Provides talks and written information conducive to developing Library volunteer interest and knowledge about library programs and services.

(continued)

Maintains volunteer computer databases for personnel files, placement, hours, and performance records and submits regular statistical summaries of volunteer activities to the Library Director. Monitors volunteer services expenditures and budget items. Provides comparative value-added summaries of volunteer District-wide contributions.

Assists staff in marketing library services and programs throughout the County.

REQUIREMENTS: Extensive knowledge of volunteer administration principles and practices necessary to manage a volunteer services program, especially in a library environment. Knowledge of volunteer recruitment and program marketing techniques. Ability to establish and maintain effective working relationships with diverse staff, managers, volunteers, and representatives of outside agencies. Skilled in oral and written communication and demonstrated ability in making public presentations. Ability to exercise sound, independent judgment finding practical solutions in a variety of personnel and program situations. Able to work a flexible schedule.

DIFFICULTY OF WORK/CONSEQUENCE OF ERROR: Work is characterized by independent planning, originality, and imagination to devise, develop, and coordinate an effective volunteer services program. Errors in work or judgment could cause interpersonal conflicts between staff and volunteers, procedural errors and disruptions in providing library services, or have a negative impact on patron and community relations.

RESPONSIBILITY: Works independently under general policy guidance and direction of the Personnel Manager. Responsible for the overall administration of the volunteer services program. Must maintain high standards of ethics and public service. May direct work of volunteers.

WORKING CONDITIONS: Primary work is performed in an office environment with extensive telephone contacts. Part of the workday is spent on a computer terminal. Usually works on multiple tasks, different software programs, and special projects during the course of a workday.

PERSONAL RELATIONSHIPS: Work involves daily contact with volunteers, staff, and representatives of community groups involving the exchange of routine and non-routine information. Represents the District to various community groups and potential volunteers.

MINIMUM QUALIFICATIONS AND SPECIAL SKILLS REQUIRED AND RESTRICTIONS

Physical: Position requires ability to work in an office environment and manage the stresses of numerous telephone calls and interruptions.

Computer Knowledge: Requires knowledge of word processing software.

Education: Minimum high school diploma or equivalent.

AND

Experience: Some administrative experience in public service work, preferably in a public library.

OR

An equivalent combination of education and experience.

WEEKLY EMPLOYMENT HOURS: 20 hours a week.

VOLUNTEER TRAINING AND ORIENTATION

For a very small program, volunteer orientation may consist of a one-on-one session with a tour of the library followed by introductions to the staff and management, and ending with a quick explanation of some specific task instructions. Training is complete. As your program expands to include other departments, or the tasks become more complex, you will need to develop more extensive orientation and training approaches (see part 3, "Training and Development").

If you cannot do all the training, whom can you assign to this task? What specific staff members have the interest, expertise, or patience to be good teachers? How will you get the cooperation of the department or branch manager to allow a staff member the time to train a volunteer?

As you set up the program, think about how volunteer training will be accomplished in a positive and productive manner.

VOLUNTEER COMMUNICATION AND FEEDBACK

Volunteers are as interested as staff in knowing what is happening in the library. Will you have a volunteer bulletin board, or will volunteers receive copies of a staff newsletter? Will you send out a bimonthly letter or will you communicate primarily through a volunteer e-mail account?

Sometimes as your time is taken up with setting up procedures, recruitment, or training, an individual volunteer may feel neglected or "out of the loop." For some people, a "hands-off" approach works out well because they enjoy being left alone to do their assigned tasks. However, others may feel isolated or unwanted and may eventually quit. It is therefore important to decide how often you (or specified staff members) will communicate with the volunteers, on what issues, and in what format. These are important considerations that should be taken into account as you set up your channels of volunteer communication.

Volunteers, on the other hand, will have comments about their experiences to share with you. It is from "the bottom up" that you gain firsthand knowledge of what is and is not working in your program.

Good communication between you, the staff, and volunteers is essential. Determine what works best in your library.

VOLUNTEER PERFORMANCE, EVALUATIONS, AND RECOGNITION

Initially, you may only have enough time to informally share a few brief comments with a volunteer about his or her work performance. For some, this is all the feedback they want or expect. There will be instances, however, when a sincere, but less skilled volunteer is not performing according to expectations. In these situations, you may wish you had a more formal evaluation process in place. The evaluation interview is a useful tool for eliciting comments from the volunteer on a personal as well as a program level and for you to discuss positive or negative issues with the volunteer.

Think about your program and picture volunteers working and enjoying their experience. Now ask yourself what you can do to give them recognition for their efforts. Will the library provide the money necessary to award and recognize these individuals? Will you have to look elsewhere for gift donations or funds? Is money available, for instance, to support a luncheon or tea? Your recognition program does not have to be elaborate or expensive, but some form of recognition is important for a successful volunteer program.

EDUCATING THE LIBRARY STAFF
ABOUT VOLUNTEERS

The library staff is not always enthused about the presence of volunteers. Even the paid staff, many of whom began their careers as library volunteers, may view your program as a threat to their positions. Others might assume that your volunteers will take all the "fun" projects and assignments.

Recognize that in financially strained libraries, the presence of volunteers may create fears that the administration is planning to replace paid positions with volunteer positions. Even when libraries are not financially threatened, the existence of volunteers places strangers into closely knit staff relationships. Moreover, if a staff member is asked to "supervise" or oversee a volunteer's work, the staff member may feel resentment because this "extra work" is not part of his or her job description. In such situations, even a hard-working volunteer may feel unwanted.

Your task is to find ways to create a team relationship between paid staff and volunteers. How will you explain to staff the introduction or expansion of your program? Who will select (or appoint) the staff members to work with volunteers? What direct benefits do you envision for an employee who agrees to do this "extra" assignment? How will you present these benefits to the staff?

You will find this aspect of volunteer administration an ongoing, fluid process that will take a lot of your time and energy. Eventually, you will be able to have the duty of "supervising volunteers" written into the job descriptions of appropriate staff. Incorporating this task is a way for library assistants or other library employees to acquire job-related supervisory skills. It also helps to establish positive relationships between paid staff and volunteers. In the interim, expect to build your program slowly on individual successes, case by case.

VALUING VOLUNTEERS

Volunteers are not free. Put on an administrative hat and ask yourself if volunteers are financially worthwhile for your library. One way to answer this question is to assign a dollar value for the volunteer hours donated on a monthly basis. Without trying to inflate your values, assign the minimum wage rate for lower skilled task hours and a percentage (such as 75 percent) of the hourly rate of individual staff for higher skilled task hours. For example, a volunteer doing five hours of basic clerical work may be worth $25.75 ($5.15/hr × 5 hours), while a volunteer doing five hours of customer computer training may be worth $45, if paid staff earn about $12 an hour ($12 × 75% × 5 hours) for similar tasks.

The program's direct costs, including your salary, volunteer supplies, forms, awards, and so forth are missing from this report. You can easily track some of these costs. Other indirect costs, such as staff and volunteer training, supervising time, time for redoing poor work, and meeting times, can only be estimated.

If you are setting up a new program (or reorganizing an existing one), you need to decide which reports and data to collect so that you can share the success of your program with management. In addition, review any existing volunteer reports for their administrative usefulness.

In the more subtle but equally important area of valuing volunteers, see what other kinds of data can be collected from conversations with customers, letters from volunteers, staff comments, or library program enhancements. This data can lend support to the value of library volunteers.

RESEARCHING VOLUNTEER INFORMATION

While setting up your program, you may need extra help or more information. There is a lot of published material on volunteer programs, but not all of it is directly applicable to libraries. Certainly this manual is a resource, as are other related publications (see the bibliography).

On a practical level, the personal contacts you make within the library community can be even more useful to your work. This work requires a phone call to other libraries to find out if they have a volunteer manager or a staff person assigned to work with or coordinate volunteers. Establishing a personal resource network early in the process of setting up your program can help you avoid some of the pitfalls that others have experienced in their programs.

A good resource network can also open up your range of program options. Discussing your program concerns with other volunteer managers can give you and other network members an opportunity to share insights, experience, and materials. It is highly unlikely that you will face any problem or dilemma with your program that was not addressed previously by someone else in your network. Members of your network can also help you to validate a new idea you want to try out in your program. Their volunteer successes can be part of your supporting data and lend credence to your new proposal. Often, library administrators want to know what other libraries have viable volunteer programs. Having success cases at your fingertips is a good way to gain the support of your administration and to demonstrate your competence in the area of library volunteerism. Finally, your resource network can serve as a source of personal support when you experience either difficult days or program successes. It is a very positive experience to share your joys and woes with others who understand what you are experiencing.

SECTION
5

Rights and Duties of Volunteers

What keeps volunteers coming back? What makes the volunteer experience a positive one for the library as well as the individual? The answers are found in the planning process. It is important to take into account the rights, responsibilities, and duties of the volunteer as a contributing member of the team and the organization.

BASIC RIGHTS IN THE WORK SITUATION

The importance of understanding the rights, responsibilities, and duties of a volunteer cannot be underestimated. Every community volunteer has a right to expect that his or her library duties represent work that:

- Is meaningful (not "make-do work") to the functioning of library operations;
- Contributes to the library's overall management plan;
- Can be completed within a reasonable time; or
- Is ongoing with tasks and duties defined by job descriptions and supported by staff expectations.

Planning the tasks and putting them into the context of library activities upgrades volunteer positions from make-do work to positive contributions.

A volunteer has the right to a designated work space. Nothing alienates someone faster than starting a job only to find out on day one that there is no place to work. A volunteer scrambling to find an appropriate work area is not only uncomfortable but counterproductive.

Finally, a volunteer has the right to some control and input over his or her assigned tasks. This input contributes to volunteer "buy in" of the project, and fosters an atmosphere of participation within the library organization.

PERSONAL RESPECT

Every community volunteer has the right to be respected as a unique individual who is contributing his or her time and energy to the library.

ORIENTATION TO THE LIBRARY

Every library volunteer has the right to a minimum training period that includes a general orientation, introductions to relevant staff, and an explanation of library policies and procedures. In addition to showing common courtesy, this practice provides volunteers with the necessary background knowledge to succeed in the organization.

The responsibility of the volunteer is to follow the established rules and polices, keep abreast of information posted on bulletin boards, read pertinent memos, and stay informed about any ongoing changes that may affect his or her work.

TRAINING

Every volunteer has the right to receive adequate training, including training in safety procedures. Additionally, the volunteer has a right to expect ongoing training and educational opportunities when appropriate. These opportunities can be used to enhance the current job or encourage an upgrade to a new position. If training costs are prohibitive, a staff member specializing in the area can be assigned to provide the training.

GRIEVANCE PROCEDURES AND CONFLICT RESOLUTION

Every volunteer has a right to air grievances during times of conflict either with another volunteer or a staff member. It is important to have a grievance procedure in place. You may use a traditional chain of command (supervisor to library director) or an open-door policy in which the volunteer manager listens to issues and makes a decision. Regardless of which method you choose to follow, the volunteer has the right to be heard.

RECOGNITION

Volunteers have a right to expect some type of recognition for the work they perform. Recognition can take the form of a simple verbal thank-you from the supervisor, a written thank-you note from the volunteer manager, or a formal luncheon or reception. The most important and enduring recognition is respect and consideration for a job well done.

Below is an example of a "Bill of Rights" for volunteers.

Rights and Duties of Volunteers

Bill of Rights for Library Volunteers

The right to adequate training for the job.

The right to be shown respect and courtesy by supervisors and staff.

The right to be informed of any information relevant to the job.

The right to a job description so that the work can be performed to the supervisor's expectations.

The right to air grievances through library volunteer channels.

The right to a job that makes a difference, a job that is meaningful and significant to the library and its customers.

The right to have some control and input over the assigned work.

The right to be recognized for contributing personal time and talent to the success of the job or project.

SECTION

6

Volunteers and Library Friends

As a volunteer manager, you may face issues relating to the role of the Library Friends' group and your role coordinating community volunteers.

In small libraries, Library Friends often serve as the backbone of the library. They are the informal group of interested individuals who operate and help fund the library. They can literally keep the doors open. Sometimes the roles of Library Friend, library volunteer, and staff overlap so closely that a member of the Friends also may be assigned "volunteer hours" working in the place of paid staff. For these people, there is little, if any, difference between roles.

In your library, the Friends organization may be chartered as a separate not-for-profit group organized under the Federal Tax Code as a 501-(c) organization. These organizations have identifiable officers, a membership list, and may send out newsletters and other information.

Alternatively, the Friends organization may be organized as a group under the umbrella of a not-for-profit library foundation. In both cases, the role of the president of the Friend's group and your role as the volunteer manager require getting people to donate their time to perform library services. Even though these are the same duties, you both "work" for separate organizations and have distinct reporting relationships.

If your library recognizes that the Friends activities are "external" to the library, for example, raising funds, managing book sales, or operating a library gift shop, you will probably have fewer conflicts. By implementing an "exclusive" voluntary policy, you can distinguish the Friends group (see sample 6-1).

Conflicts can occur if you are coordinating an individual who is both a community volunteer and a long-term member of the Friends group, or if you are asked to take over the coordination of volunteer activities in areas traditionally handled by the Friends group. To effectively manage these or other potential

The Friends meeting room is designated for Friends members' use only and will not be used by staff, community volunteers, or the general public.

Community volunteers are welcome to use all public facilities but cannot store their personal effects in the employee lockers or use the employee lounge as a break area.

Community volunteers may be invited, but not required, to become members of the Friends of the Library.

The volunteer manager is responsible for reporting hours of volunteer service performed by community volunteers and court-ordered workers. The president of the Friends group has the responsibility for tracking membership hours.

The annual Library Recognition Day will recognize staff for outstanding achievements. Recognition for community volunteers will be held during National Library Volunteer Week. The president of the Friends group is responsible for announcing the time and place of the Friends recognition event.

The public library volunteer insurance covers only community volunteers working under the direction of the volunteer manager or a designated library manager or staff person. Volunteer insurance does not cover the functions of the Friends group.

The volunteer manager will maintain the volunteer applications and personnel forms of all community volunteers. It is the responsibility of the president of the Friends group to maintain the Friends' membership records.

conflicts, consider working with the library administration to develop a set of program policies that define how these two areas of volunteerism will be addressed. The following considerations will help you write a policy.

CONSIDERATIONS IN POLICY DEVELOPMENT

Dues and Membership Requirements

Should library volunteers be required to also be members of the Library Friends group? There are volunteers who want to help the library without the obligations of attending meetings or paying dues. There are talented volunteers who may only want to work on a particular project, for example, data-based management of volunteer statistics, and not be involved in fund-raising efforts by a Friends group.

Conversely, one large metropolitan public library has a docent group whose members receive special computer training and in return give individual instruction to customers on searching the online catalog, the World Wide Web, and other library holdings. Docents are required to be paid members of the Friends group.

Another public library uses honorary membership in the Friends group as a reward to selected community volunteers who have given a minimum number of hours of volunteer service.

Tasks and Responsibilities

Who assigns volunteers to the library-related tasks that need to be done? Maintaining the community bulletin board or library displays may have been part of the Friends group efforts for years. If these tasks now come under the purview of the volunteer manager, it is important that the shift in task assignments is positively communicated to all concerned and formalized by job descriptions. When this doesn't happen, a volunteer/Friend may be caught in the middle trying to meet both the Friends' president and the volunteer manager's expectations. This situation seldom has a successful outcome.

De-volunteering and Membership

Not all individuals are suited to be library volunteers. For different reasons it may be necessary to "de-volunteer" an individual. Although it is often difficult for a volunteer manager to de-volunteer a person, it is much easier when there is a clear distinction between a community volunteer expected to work according to a number of requirements and a "dues-paying" member of the Friends group. Paying dues and attending meetings do not necessarily make a useful volunteer.

When an individual is both a community volunteer and a member of the Friends group, you must take the time to explain the distinction. Showing sensitivity to the volunteer's feelings is essential to keeping the de-volunteering process from having a negative effect on the activities of the Friends group. You may find it useful to talk over the situation with the library manager and the president of the Friends to see if there is another assignment the volunteer can be given within the Friends' scope of activities.

Volunteer Hours and Rules

How will the hours of community volunteers and Friends be reported? Do the hours attending a Friends meeting count the same as the hours worked by a community volunteer doing her assigned tasks? Should the Friends' time count only for special events, such as the time preparing for and managing a book sale? Are both types of hours assigned a dollar valuation?

A community volunteer can be required to follow the rules in completing a time form or a sign-in sheet. On the other hand, there are dedicated, hard-working members of the Friends who feel they should not take credit for the many hours they contribute to the library. They refuse to complete time forms. As a practical consequence, their hours of service will be either omitted or at best underestimated on volunteer service reports.

Recognition and Awards

Will community volunteers and Friends receive the same kinds of awards and recognition? Will the two groups come together for recognition events? Consider that longevity for community volunteers is usually measured in months, while in some Friends groups, longevity is measured in years. Would recognition be given for "years of service" or "the level of accomplishment of a task" or both? An inclusive policy is provided at sample 6-2.

Further, some Friends groups use part of their dues to support special awards for their members. Some public libraries have no budget for volunteer recognition or awards. This discrepancy in funding could lead to difficulties trying to make a combined recognition event a positive experience for everyone. You may decide that separate functions held at different times of the year may work better.

The perceived status differences between long-standing library Friends and newer community volunteers can also cause some difficulties if not handled diplomatically. Giving the same type of honors (flowers, pins, plaques, etc.) or trying to select a "Volunteer of the Year" from members of both groups may create more problems than satisfying rewards.

Risk Management and Volunteers

Some public libraries carry special volunteer insurance as part of their overall insurance program. Volunteers are not covered by workers' compensation when injured on the job, and the volunteer insurance can cover medical costs if an accident occurs. As a volunteer manager, you can ask a volunteer to provide a police report and proof of automobile insurance if the assigned duties require the use of a vehicle, such as home delivery of library books.

On the other hand, Friends groups are usually separate, nonprofit organizations. A member would not be covered by the library's volunteer insurance if he were working on an assignment for the Friends. For example, if a Friend volunteer is injured while moving books for a book sale, he would not necessarily be reimbursed for

Library volunteers include all individuals who voluntarily give their time and talents to help further the mission of the public library in providing materials and information to our community. Included here are trustees, library Friends, docents, and community adult and youth volunteers.

Members of the library Friends and local volunteers are equally important in enhancing the efforts of the public library's paid staff in providing outstanding library service.

Library community volunteers and Friends of the Library are considered by the public library as unpaid staff and are included in all library activities and share in all nonmonetary benefits and facility use that is open to all staff.

Library community volunteers are considered an integral part of the library staff and can use the lockers, break room, and kitchen facilities.

For administrative reporting, all community service volunteer hours, including those of court-ordered workers, will be reported on a monthly basis.

Volunteer hours include any hours contributed for the betterment of the public library, whether on- or off-site, whether a community volunteer, Friends member, or court-ordered worker. Hours will be collected and reported to the library director on a monthly basis.

The public library's annual recognition event will award staff, community volunteers, and Friends of the Library.

medical costs. A community volunteer injured while doing the same assignment could file a medical claim under the special volunteer insurance. As you can see, it is important to clarify your particular situation with the risk manager of your library.

Library Space

Does the library support a separate Friends meeting room, lockers, book storage space, display space, and so forth within the library building? Can community volunteers use the room, space, or lockers? Are your community volunteers treated more like paid staff, Friends members, or neither when they store their personal effects, take breaks, or perform duties?

The degree of exclusivity and "control" over library space is a subtle issue that can affect the feelings of all those involved. In very small libraries where all space is viewed as a shared commodity, tensions may be minimal. As defined space becomes informally or formally allocated, the volunteer manager may have to negotiate space usage between the respective groups.

In larger library systems, Friends groups may use a separate building for meetings and other activities, such as operating a used bookstore or a used clothing shop. When this occurs, Friends and community volunteers will usually evolve into very separate entities and may have little contact with each other.

Library Perks

As you view the two groups, are different perks or privileges given to members of the Friends that are not given to community volunteers or vice versa? Are the perks closer to those received by paid, part-time, or regular staff?

Perks for either group may include waivers on fines, opportunities to check out new best-sellers first, the privilege of additional renewals, or the opportunity to order books through the library purchasing department. If community volunteers and Friends members have been physically separated over time, the issue of differential perks is less important to all parties.

SECTION
7

Legal and Risk Management Issues

The legal concerns of a library volunteer program closely parallel those associated with the employment of paid staff. Included in this section are:

Volunteer recruiting and discrimination issues;

Recruiting and ADA practices;

Developmentally disabled volunteers;

Recruitment of youth;

Youth at-risk volunteers;

Volunteerism and court-ordered workers;

Driving records and auto insurance;

Hiring and health and safety regulations;

General safety training;

Workers' compensation;

Customer confidentiality;

De-volunteering;

The Good Samaritan Act and volunteers; and

Volunteer insurance.

The legal and risk management issues surrounding the use of volunteers can seem overwhelming at first, but are actually quite manageable when broken down into specific areas of concern. However, your first decision is how your library defines the term *volunteers*. If you adhere strictly to the set of library hiring guidelines, volunteers can be considered unpaid staff and their "employment" must meet the required standards for paid employees.

On the other hand, a distinction can be made between paid staff and volunteers. In this case, the paid staff meet employment standards, but there are no rules for "hiring" volunteers. You need early clarification about how your key administrators (e.g., library director, risk manager, insurance broker, or attorney) want you to approach the "hiring" and "employment" of library volunteers.

VOLUNTEER RECRUITING AND DISCRIMINATION ISSUES

When recruiting volunteers, you are not legally required to advertise or post your positions to meet affirmative action standards. However, you may be asked to follow the library hiring guidelines in posting or advertising volunteer opportunities.

Even if your library does not require strict hiring compliance, you want to be sensitive to the public relations problems that could occur if someone made the charge that the local library discriminated against certain types of volunteers (e.g., the disabled, specific racial minorities, etc.). The burden of proof would be on you and the library administration to show that this wasn't the case.

There is a balancing act in employing good volunteers. You definitely want to hold to the philosophy of recruiting the best volunteer from the available pool of applicants for every position. Yet you may have an obligation to honor the requests of departmental managers (your internal customers), who do not want to have particular types of volunteers in their specific areas of operation. For example, an obese individual with good telephone skills wants to apply for an information desk position. She is willing to volunteer two nights a week at the times needed. The library manager, however, feels that this individual does not present a professional image and wants you to find someone else.

If the administration wants you to follow the library's legal employment guidelines, obesity is not an EEOC/affirmative action issue. Nonetheless, it can come under the jurisdiction of the Americans with Disability Act (ADA), depending on the individual's medical circumstances. You have a willing and able volunteer who can do the assigned tasks. How would you handle this situation? First, make sure there is a well-prepared job description specifying the skills and competencies for the information desk position. This document helps you to provide a basis for objective decision making in matching the individual's skills with the task requirements. It also serves as a basis for administrative review in the event a conflict resolution process is required.

Second, recognize that the library manager generally has the right to decide who works in her department or area of responsibility. The balancing act requires that you apply your talents in educating and persuading the manager that you have identified the best-qualified volunteer for the position. Negotiate with the library manager to set up a trial period with a specific end date to evaluate how the volunteer is working out in the position. At the same time, you may be able to offer suggestions to the volunteer by focusing on the public image aspects of the job.

RECRUITING AND ADA PRACTICES

The Americans with Disabilities Act (ADA) (1990) does not address volunteers per se, although some library systems apply the same rules to volunteers as to paid staff. If volunteers come into the library as customers, they fall under the public accommodation section of the ADA. However, if they work in the library as volunteers, they are exempt from the act.

Beyond the strict legal interpretations, you may have disabled volunteers apply for positions. Here again, your willingness to make "reasonable accommodations" in the workplace demonstrates a good faith effort on the part of the library organization to use the talents of disabled individuals.

Disabled volunteers are often willing to help you in adapting tasks to fit their requirements. In doing this, they are actually helping the library organization learn how to make reasonable accommodations, as required by law, in the event a staff member becomes disabled or a disabled individual is hired.

DEVELOPMENTALLY DISABLED VOLUNTEERS

The broad heading of disability includes adolescents and young adults who are developmentally disabled or brain injured. They are in special "return to work" programs. A job coach from a private rehabilitation company may contact you to see if you are willing to work with a developmentally disabled individual in a nonpaid volunteer position. The rehabilitation facility is usually paid by either an insurance company or funded through a state or federal program to assist these individuals in finding gainful employment.

When the job coach calls you, set up an interview. This is to make sure there are no hidden agendas (such as the expectation of a paying job, see paragraph below) and that the individual has the skills necessary to perform the available work. Do not be too quick to prejudge the type of tasks that the disabled person can or cannot do.

If your goal is to provide a volunteer opportunity for the disabled individual to gain skills, confidence, and experience in a work setting, or merely to enable the person to get out and be among people, you may be able to assist the individual if the appropriate library tasks are available. If there is an expectation that the individual will move into a regular, paid position at some future date, it is very important that this decision be coordinated with the human resources department and the library manager. Library employment guidelines and the authorization to fill a position may be outside your scope of authority as a volunteer manager. If the individual transfers to either a part- or full-time position that is eventually downsized or eliminated, the library may face additional administrative and legal concerns.

Therefore, during your initial interview, talk with the job coach and the volunteer. Explain that if a position opens up, the volunteer is welcome to apply, but all hiring is based on a pool of applicants and no special preference is given. The hiring manager may review the volunteer's performance records as part of the hiring process, but this is only one factor among many that may be considered.

You may need to be sensitive to potential prejudices among the library staff and managers about having developmentally disabled individuals working in the library, either in a volunteer or paid position. This prejudice should not limit your efforts in working with the disabled because bringing these individuals into the library system supports employment diversity policies and can benefit everyone.

Finally, it is important to know how much time the job coach will be on-site at your library and how much time will be committed to working directly with the disabled individual. The more time the job coach is willing to commit, the more likely the success of the experience.

RECRUITMENT OF YOUTH

Youth (ages thirteen to eighteen) may want to volunteer to complete graduation requirements or meet a service group requirement (e.g., for the Scouts). Others may want to volunteer to gain experience for a future part-time position as a library page, or a staff member may ask you to find a volunteer position for a daughter or son.

There are two sets of quasi-legal issues when working with young people. First, there are state employment regulations governing the employment of youth and the hours they may work. As volunteers, these youth do not come under these statutes, but these regulations may serve as excellent guidelines on the times and hours you can use them. For example, if the state law does not allow a sixteen-year-old (or younger) teenager to work after 7:00 P. M. on a school night, you can use this as a guide to determine appropriate hours for any volunteers under sixteen years of age.

The second quasi-legal area is the consent of a parent or legal guardian to work. If your library employs sixteen-year-olds in staff positions without requiring consent forms, you can use this as the basis for your own policy. Therefore, any volunteer under the age of sixteen would be required to submit a consent form.

The parts of a consent form are simple and should include the following points: tasks, safety or health issues, scheduled times, and the signature of the parent or legal guardian agreeing to let their teenager perform volunteer work at the library. If an accident happens, there is shared liability with the parents.

Additionally, the consent form serves the purpose of clarifying the role of the teenager in the context of the library: all volunteer positions carry task expectations. If the youth does not perform, you have a basis for notifying the parent or legal guardian and de-volunteering their child.

It is important to establish a minimum age limit for accepting young volunteers. Sometimes adolescents do not have the maturity to work in a structured environment without close supervision. If you decide to take a volunteer younger than fifteen for any reason, make sure a parent will be close by to help supervise the child's activity. Consider the case of a nine-year-old who was caught throwing stones in the school yard and assigned to do two hours of community service by the principal. The parents asked the volunteer manager if their child could volunteer at the library to meet the principal's requirement. An exception was made as long as one of the parents stayed on-site.

YOUTH AT-RISK VOLUNTEERS

Within the category of youth volunteers is the more specific area of Youth at Risk. These young people often have serious problems at school, are in trouble with the law, or both. It takes a special approach and a lot of patience to work with them. Successfully using this type of volunteer in the library usually involves setting task expectations, giving positive reinforcement, providing proper supervision and challenging tasks, and showing individualized interest.

Keep in mind that if you or a staff person cannot give these young people the attention they require, you might think twice about hiring them as volunteers.

VOLUNTEERISM AND COURT-ORDERED WORKERS

The local court systems are using community service as part of the restitution process for individuals convicted of relatively minor offenses. Court-ordered individuals can include both youth offenders and adults. The formal paperwork originates from the local court and stipulates the number of hours ordered for restitution; it often includes a secondary time sheet to show the actual hours and days worked.

In some library systems, a library manager or department head may be responsible for court-ordered community service workers and the volunteer manager responsible for only community volunteers. In others, the volunteer manager coordinates both kinds of "volunteers."

If you are assigned to work with court-ordered volunteers, check with the court liaison to make sure these workers are covered by the city or county court insurance while working on library property. In most cases, the court coverage will apply. You may also want to make sure they are covered after the date shown on the court form. For example, Jimmy is supposed to have all of his assigned restitution hours completed by the fifteenth of the month as shown on the form. He calls you with car problems two days earlier and promises to complete his hours on the sixteenth. If Jimmy has an accident at the library on the sixteenth, will the court insurance cover him? Find out before you agree to extend his completion date.

When you use court-ordered or community service volunteers, establish a firm policy on the types of offenses you will accept. Most libraries will take people convicted of Driving Under the Influence (DUIs), Driving While Intoxicated (DWIs), and minor traffic infractions (e.g., no automobile insurance, speeding, excess parking tickets), truancy, and possession of a controlled substance. They will not accept individuals who commit crimes such as robbery, purse snatching, stealing, or similar offenses. You have a right to ask the nature of the offense, to accept or reject the individual, and an obligation to maintain confidentiality of this information.

You also have a right to enforce library standards of dress, behavior, and task expectations for these individuals. There will be some individuals who think the library is an easy place to complete their community service and think you have the obligation to meet their demands concerning times and tasks. This is not the case. If an individual is not performing his or her assigned tasks, does not show up on schedule, or leaves early, you have the right to terminate the relationship immediately.

POLICE REPORTS, BACKGROUND, AND REFERENCE CHECKS

If your volunteers are going to represent the library off the premises (such as delivering books to individuals in their homes), it is prudent to have a policy that requires a police report or background check. In highly transient urban or suburban areas, this procedure shows a good faith effort on the part of the library to employ "safe" volunteers.

Contacting the people listed as references for a potential volunteer is useful for getting background information. If the referral or reference is from another library or a small nonprofit agency, the individual contacted may be a very good source for sharing information. Larger agencies and private employers, concerned about lawsuits, may not be as free to discuss information about the individual.

If you decide to check references, you must be consistent for all positions, or at least for anyone who applies for specific volunteer positions such as homebound delivery of books. Consistency is important in preventing impressions of favoritism or opening yourself to accusations of showing a pattern of discriminatory behavior.

The questions used in a reference check should be focused on the specific volunteer job duties and position behaviors. If you want someone with good computer skills to work on database management for the library, you can ask about computer skills. However, it is inappropriate to ask about the individual's public speaking skills because they are not required for the job. In a similar manner, you can ask about the individual's commitment to meeting scheduled times, but it is inappropriate to ask if the individual has a sick parent at home who might affect his or her schedule because the latter has nothing to do with performing the job.

Taking time to prepare appropriate questions for your volunteer positions and reviewing them with a key administrator can prevent potential problems related to hiring.

DRIVING RECORDS AND AUTO INSURANCE

For any position that requires a volunteer to drive a personal vehicle, it is prudent to ask to see both a current motor vehicle record (MVR) and proof of automobile insurance. Make copies of each one to keep in the volunteer's file.

If a review of the driving record shows a DUI or a high number of points, you have sufficient reason to disqualify the applicant from a position that requires driving for the library. If there is an accident while the volunteer is on library business, the library could become party to a lawsuit in the event of injuries or heavy property damage.

Do not assign a volunteer to drive a library-owned vehicle without first checking with the appropriate administrator or insurance broker. The volunteer is not paid staff and the insurance may not cover anyone not employed by the library system. Always check first.

Finally, once a year, review your records for volunteers assigned to driving positions. Always keep updated copies of insurance and license information for your records. If you or a staff member feel there is a potential problem, you can order an MVR on behalf of the library to see if there has been some deterioration in the driving record.

HIRING AND HEALTH AND SAFETY REGULATIONS

Public libraries do not fall under the Occupational Health and Safety Act (OSHA), but corporate libraries do. The "Right to Know" regulations are useful guidelines that let people in the workplace know what chemicals are present and give them access to Material Safety Data Sheets (MSDS). This would include volunteers.

Libraries have numerous quantities of cleaners, solvents, book mending glues, and so forth. For most individuals, these chemicals are not a problem. For a few chemically sensitive people, coming into contact with any chemical may cause allergic reactions.

In your job descriptions, informal task cards, or task lists, it is important to accurately detail any potential health and safety issues, especially if the individual is going to use cleaning solvents or insecticides.

The safety administrator can help you interpret the information in an MSDS and show you where these sheets are located in the library.

GENERAL SAFETY TRAINING

It is important not to fall into the habit of assuming that volunteers will use their common sense in performing assigned tasks. A volunteer may prop a ladder against the wall next to a large window and reach toward the window to water the hanging plants. This is an accident waiting to happen. From the viewpoint of the volunteer, this is the way it's done at home. In terms of risk management, you cannot assume that volunteers will be aware of safety and liability issues as they affect the library. In addition, many volunteers receive a cursory overview of job expectations, with little or no attention paid to safety concerns. Safety is often seen as secondary to the volunteer starting work as quickly as possible. As the volunteer manager, you have an obligation to be aware of any health and safety issues as well as the emergency procedures associated with all assigned tasks. You or a staff member can orientate the volunteer about safety concerns, including the proper use of equipment.

WORKERS' COMPENSATION

Although a volunteer cannot file a workers' compensation claim for on-the-job injuries or illnesses (only paid staff can do this), the library's medical portion of the general liability insurance will probably be the source of funds if a claim is made against the library by an injured volunteer.

For example, Judy is carrying a box of books to the donation area for sorting. On the way, she trips and hits her head against the steel shelving and the wound bleeds profusely. There are several possible scenarios that the staff can follow after this type of incident. Someone can go through Judy's purse for her medical card and call her health carrier for instructions; call a relative and let one of them take her to a clinic or doctor; or call 911 and let them make the decision. If you take her to the library's designated workers' compensation clinic, her health insurance carrier may not cover the claim. In this case, you would probably want to file the claim with your general liability insurance carrier under the medical portion of the plan.

This kind of situation underscores the importance of having a written policy on emergencies involving volunteers. You can work with the library safety officer in designing guidelines so that the staff is clear about what to do in the event of an accident.

Preventing volunteer-initiated accidents is critical. This is where your ability as a manager comes into play. You need to learn how to monitor what the volunteers are doing and how they are performing their tasks.

CUSTOMER CONFIDENTIALITY

The library rules governing customer confidentiality should be a part of any volunteer training, especially the training of those working at or near the circulation desk or accessing the computer records of library customers.

A volunteer may overhear a staff member make inappropriate comments about someone's book-reading habits. It is important to instruct the volunteer that this information is confidential and cannot be divulged to anyone, including family members. The extra few minutes you take to explain this policy may pay off later.

TERMINATION INTERVIEWS

A volunteer may leave with or without notice. If notice is given, ideally you may want to schedule a termination interview. This technique is usually a good way to learn about your program from the "bottom up" and find ways to improve it. When volunteers leave on friendly terms, they are often willing to share their ideas on how to make the library a better volunteer experience.

DE-VOLUNTEERING

In a formal de-volunteering, it is important to review the situation with a trusted administrator. Are there other options to consider? For example, a volunteer is slow in completing the assigned tasks. Is there another type of work that might be more appropriate? If a volunteer is not getting along with a particular staff member or another volunteer, is there another time or part of the building they can work? Are your facts accurate?

Can you counsel the volunteer about other agencies or explore an individual interest that allows the volunteer to leave you and the library on good terms? Has the individual just been through a major life crisis (e.g., loss of a spouse) that affects his or her work or staff relationships? Does he or she need some time away from the library? A decision to de-volunteer requires careful preparation including consideration of any possible legal ramifications.

GOOD SAMARITAN ACT AND VOLUNTEERS

The Federal Volunteer Protection Act of 1997 grants immunity from personal liability to volunteers in nonprofit and government organizations who are acting within the scope of their duties. This new law covers volunteers in public libraries as a government organization and the Friends of the Library as a nonprofit, 501-(c) organization. In addition to this federal law, all fifty states have laws that limit the personal liability for volunteers.

Under a typical good samaritan act, volunteers are protected from personal liability when they act in good faith, or make honest mistakes because of something they did or did not do. For example, a volunteer reading in the children's section gives medical assistance during a medical emergency. For some reason, the parents decide to sue the library and the volunteer. The library and the volunteer find legal relief under the good samaritan act. Note that volunteers are not protected from willful misconduct, crimes of violence, committing a sexual offense, or violating someone's civil liberties.

Check with your library attorney on the applicable state law and the interpretation of the Federal Volunteer Protection Act as they affect your program.

VOLUNTEER INSURANCE

A library system can purchase inexpensive volunteer insurance to provide additional coverage for volunteers in the areas of accident, individual liability, and automobile liability. For example, if a volunteer is involved in an auto accident while driving to a customer's home to deliver books, the additional automobile coverage could provide added protection to the library in the event of a claim or if the liability limits are reached on the volunteer's automobile insurance.

Ask your library insurance broker whether purchasing this coverage would be worthwhile for your library.

SECTION

8

Volunteer Program Communication

There are several methods or channels of communicating information within the library organization and to and from the local community. Learning to use these channels effectively is important for the volunteer manager to develop a successful volunteer program. In particular, the following factors need to be taken into consideration:

The flow of information and information networks;

The communication environment;

Effective communication channels;

Volunteer communication channels; and

Communication feedback.

THE FLOW OF INFORMATION AND INFORMATION NETWORKS

Every library has an internal communication environment that silently defines the dominant directions and patterns in the flow of information. In some libraries, staff can directly e-mail or send a memo to the library director without providing a copy to their supervisor. In others, memos and announcements come from the top down, and only supervisors can send written correspondence to higher levels of management. In still others, communication can be sent and received diagonally throughout the organization, thus tying together staff and managers in different departments, locations, and authority levels. At one end of the spectrum, the flow of communication is open and easy while in others communication is closed and restrained.

THE COMMUNICATION ENVIRONMENT

New volunteer managers might not understand the existing communication networks and therefore hesitate to use them. If you are in a split position with the management of volunteers as only one part of your workload, you will have to step back and assess the networks from your two roles. In one role, for example as reference librarian, all communication may have to follow the chain of command through your immediate supervisor, but in your role as volunteer manager, a variety of internal and external networks may be available to you.

To assess your library's communication environment, review the written correspondence you have received. Is there a distinct sequence or ordering of names on the memos or internal correspondence? Is there a standard listing of people in the library who receive carbon copies of all communications? You will be more successful following the already established networks. However, if there is ambiguity or you are in a loosely structured organization, this situation can work to your advantage if you take the initiative to establish new networks that are useful to you in your role as volunteer manager. For example, establishing a resource network of staff and managers you can contact, regardless of their formal positions, is advantageous in helping you discover new jobs for volunteers. There are also individuals and groups in the community who can help you recruit volunteers.

EFFECTIVE COMMUNICATION CHANNELS

Communication channels can be divided into written and verbal formats. Written communication refers to general or confidential memos, letters to managers or library board members, volunteer forms, form letters, newsletters, position announcements, handbooks, directives, certificates, spreadsheets, budget request forms, e-mail, and faxes. It also includes graphics on pressboard, notes on white boards, comments in the margins of letters or memos, the use of flip charts, writing on overhead transparencies, and Web page postings. All of these are ways you can send and receive information to individuals or groups through the formal or informal networks within your library. Few people, however, communicate effectively in all of these mediums. Poorly written or inappropriate communication can lead to problems. The cryptic note in the margin of a memo can do more immediate communication damage than a poorly written volunteer form. A difficult-to-read note scribbled on the volunteer information board can lead to minor misunderstanding, while a widely circulated e-mail message written in anger can have ramifications for weeks. A formal style of communication, while appropriate for staff, can be viewed as cold and uncaring when sent to a sensitive volunteer.

Oral communication can include face-to-face conversations with volunteers, community members, staff, and managers in either an individual or group setting. It can also include day-to-day pleasantries and acknowledgments, grapevine and scuttlebutt conversations, task instructions, telephone conversations, voice mail, videotape presentations, and the "reading" of nonverbal messages. The subtleties of verbal communication can be distorted when you accidentally fail to acknowledge a volunteer starting a shift, or your voice on the telephone is wrongly interpreted.

There are books and instructional guides available on written and oral forms of communication covering appropriate techniques, styles, limitations, and etiquette. You can build the necessary skillsets to become a competent communicator with practice, patience, and some trial and error effort. At the beginning, identify the staff you think are effective communicators and pattern your style after theirs until you gain the confidence to develop your own style.

COMMUNICATION WITH VOLUNTEERS

The individual community member's first contact with you may be through a written announcement or a Web page posting for a position. At this point there is no face-to-face contact, yet you have successfully communicated information. In another situation, a potential volunteer may have picked up an application form and sent it to you. Again, you may have had no personal contact with the individual, yet information is being communicated to you in writing. Impressions are formed during this initial phase on the basis of these written materials.

Most impressions and judgments (correct or incorrect) are made during the first two to three minutes of an initial conversation. You are deciding whether or not this individual may make a good volunteer and the candidate is deciding whether to work with you. In an important way, you are in a public relations role as a representative of the library. Even if the conversation goes no further than the initial meeting, your communication approach and style will leave an impression and reflect on the library organization.

In the formal interview phase of recruitment, oral communication includes the skills of active listening to what is and is not said. The use of a written job description or task card can help clarify the points you make about the job. Your openness in sharing the positive and negative aspects of the position and your ability to interpret the nonverbal communication are all part of the mutual clarification process.

It is important that the staff person assigned to supervise the volunteer has good oral skills to accurately explain what is required and the patience to review the job task list. As the volunteer continues to work, the supervisor must have the verbal skills to provide feedback for his or her effort and give positive reinforcement for a job well done. This nurtures the volunteer's ego and encourages volunteer loyalty to the library and the department. Along the same lines, day-to-day pleasantries and acknowledgment by name provide additional reinforcements.

Effective communication with the volunteer staff is in part determined by the size of your volunteer pool and in part by your own communication style. A small number of volunteers can be informed of policy changes, special events, and training opportunities through informal meetings, special notices on bulletin boards, or a personal telephone call. As the number of volunteers increases, these forms of communication can be augmented by a monthly or quarterly newsletter, memos to each volunteer, a formal monthly or quarterly meeting, or perhaps even the use of e-mail or faxed messages. Throughout the year, a personal meeting with each volunteer periodically lets you know how the program is working and what each person feels about his or her volunteer experience.

COMMUNICATION FEEDBACK

Many managers think that if they talk to a staff person or send a memo or an e-mail message, the communication is understood and acted on according to their intent. It is easy to fall into this trap as a volunteer manager. Receiving communication does not mean that a person understands the message. Understanding a message does not mean that a person agrees with it. Agreeing with the message does not mean that a person will act in the same way that the manager intended.

Volunteers can experience additional difficulties because they are approaching your oral and written messages from widely different communication contexts. Telling a volunteer that she or he will be cleaning books may easily create the image of a large pail of soapy water. To ask a volunteer to put the books in order on a cart may be interpreted as ordering them by size or color and not by the Dewey Decimal System. Most of the messaging done within a library organization is based on an implicit understanding that is in turn based on the staff's contextual knowledge of the way things get done.

A major component in communication is completing the information loop, which is accomplished by getting feedback on the messages you send. In the simplest case, you can ask a volunteer to repeat and explain what she heard. For example, you can say, "Explain to me how you will go about copying and collating this twenty-page handout." You can listen to the explanation to determine if the volunteer understood the instructions on operating the copier and how to do two-sided copying.

During a volunteer meeting, you may see heads nodding as part of the nonverbal behavior of participants but this does not mean that you are getting agreement on a set of actions. You can get feedback by asking questions and getting the members' opinions and commitments on who will undertake which actions and when. You can also follow up with individuals after a meeting either in person or by telephone and encourage them to ask questions about topics or concerns that they are still not sure about. Here, too, silence does not necessarily mean understanding, agreement, or action.

The margins on memos and letters are useful spaces to seek clarifications. For example, a volunteer writes you a memo on a possible community service project. Before meeting with the individual, you can give him or her feedback by writing questions in the margins such as, "How many hours will this take?" "Do you know anyone else who is interested?" "Is there a financial cost to the library?" and then send the memo back. This shows your interest and allows the individual time to provide clarification of the proposed project so that your meeting time becomes more effective. Even if the project does not materialize, the volunteer can feel you were interested and understood what the proposal was all about.

Another way to get feedback is to establish action dates on your calendar and then check back to see if the activities that were to be accomplished were actually done. Hearing the words "everything is fine" does not necessarily mean that everything is fine.

Exit interviews and exit surveys are ways to acquire feedback about the volunteer program and the individual volunteer experience. A volunteer moving out of state or returning to full-time employment is likely to share honest opinions about the program. This is important feedback.

If your library allows volunteers to have e-mail accounts on your computer system, you can request and give communication feedback. Let your volunteers know that sending information through electronic methods (e-mail, voice mail, and faxes) is not confidential.

Finally, the completion of good communication feedback is based on your ability to keep the informal and formal networks open and your willingness to accept and hear positive and negative comments.

Program Communication Guidelines

The following are intended to facilitate the flow of good communication.

1. There are three types of networks available to transmit information: oral, written, and electronic. Which one you use is determined by the audience, availability of equipment, the urgency of the information, the size of the staff, and the type of information being communicated.

2. Top management needs to recognize the importance of good communication at all levels and create an environment to encourage it.

3. Keep channels of communication open by encouraging feedback, especially through question-and-answer periods at the end of meetings, follow-up meetings, and written comments on memos.

4. Written communication includes job descriptions, memos, staff and volunteer newsletters, and policy and procedure manuals.

5. Oral communication includes group and individual meetings, exit interviews, orientation, and training.

6. Electronic communication includes e-mail, voice mail, and faxes. It is important to remember that information sent through electronic channels is not confidential.

7. Volunteers need feedback through verbal and written comments not only about their work, but to show concern for them as individuals.

8. Volunteers need clear and concise written and oral task instruction so that they can successfully complete the job.

9

Volunteer Program Evaluation

Successful volunteer programs require some level of evaluation, even if you conduct the evaluation on an informal basis. In putting together a program evaluation, consider the following six areas:

1. Administrative support;
2. Community satisfaction;
3. Staff satisfaction;
4. Volunteer satisfaction;
5. Individual program satisfaction; and
6. Volunteer manager satisfaction.

ADMINISTRATIVE SUPPORT

Do you have administrative support for the volunteer program? What kind of information would key administrators like to have to feel comfortable with the program or to consider it successful? Without hesitation, they would want the statistics generated from the time donated by volunteers. By incorporating these into regular reports, you can demonstrate the financial worth of your program to the overall operation of the library. In addition, adding narratives about the accomplishments of volunteers or how they affect specific services reinforces and drives home the success of your program. Finally, discuss with your supervisor other reporting options that will highlight your program.

COMMUNITY SATISFACTION

Informally, a successful program produces verbal comments of thanks and expressed feelings of satisfaction from recipients. Customers who are part of "read-aloud" programs, whether at retirement homes, nursing homes, or day-care centers, are often very appreciative of the efforts of library volunteers. Use these comments to document your success and consider them part of your evaluation feedback. Make quick notes of these comments for your evaluation file, noting the date, place, and person making the comments. Eventually these can become part of your overall program evaluation at the end of the year.

In addition, written letters of appreciation sent to the library director, the letters-to-the-editor section of the local newspaper, or to your office over the course of a year are useful documents that demonstrate the qualitative level of satisfaction for specific programs. In some instances, you can solicit letters from the directors of service facilities, such as senior centers, that show their support and appreciation for the library volunteers.

If the library sponsors a community recognition event for volunteers, the number of people who attend can be an indicator of support. Are community leaders, such as the mayor and city manager, present? Did your guest list include the press or electronic media and library customers? Did they receive special invitations?

Be careful about interpreting community and customer indicators of support. Newspapers do not always publish letters to the editor because of lack of space or other factors. Conflicting schedules may prevent key community leaders from attending a volunteer function. Weather conditions, community events (e.g., high school homecomings) can also lower the attendance. Nevertheless, make informative notes in your file. These notes can serve as future planning guides and provide information for writing your program evaluation.

STAFF SATISFACTION

How does the staff evaluate your program? Depending on their prior experiences or on a particular staff member, the initial response to volunteers may be to see them as a necessary evil. You may hear, "Yes, some volunteers are useful and know what they are doing, but in general, volunteers get in our way, mess up our procedures, and take time supervising. They may replace us."

A key factor in the success of the volunteer program is neutralizing negative comments by, and even better, making supporters of the staff.

To have an individual express negative comments about volunteers and then turn around a year later and become your strongest supporter is an excellent indicator of the growing acceptance of your program. Other indicators include the number of staff who willingly offer to supervise or work with volunteers and identify useful volunteer projects or tasks. If a workshop on supervising volunteers is offered, the number of staff signing up to attend would be indicative of staff support, as would identifying the extra work that gets done.

VOLUNTEER SATISFACTION

Volunteers who are satisfied with their library experience will talk to you, the staff, and their friends. They sell your program. Satisfied volunteers often express a positive feeling at being part of the library team, offer to train other volunteers, and take on tasks that others do not want to do. There will be some volunteers who will take time to write thank-you notes and comments about how much they enjoy volunteering at the library. Save these notes. In addition, take informal notes about the positive verbal comments you

receive. These can be added to your program evaluation file.

Volunteers who have a mildly positive experience are not likely to discuss their feelings. They may be generally satisfied with their assignment because they feel their skills are being used to serve their community. To get a response from one of these individuals, you may need to have a one-on-one interview or send out a short survey to capture their comments.

When a program seems disorganized with no

volunteer orientation, limited staff support, little or no training, vague task expectations, negative staff comments, no assigned work space, or no place for personal items, then negative feelings will often translate into increased absenteeism and the loss of volunteers. This too can be a basis for evaluating your program. Attempt to talk to these volunteers. They may provide you with information for reevaluating your policies, procedures, communications, and staff-volunteer relationships. In the end, you may find that overall you have a highly satisfied group with the exception of one department, task area, or one or two individuals. Although small in number, the negative individuals may choose to complain to anyone who will listen rather than find other volunteer opportunities in the community.

Monitoring volunteer satisfaction on a regular basis is a good way to maintain the quality of your program. Use the Volunteer Program Evaluation Checklist (sample 9-1) to provide feedback for your program.

INDIVIDUAL PROGRAM SATISFACTION

Keeping statistics and writing up successful volunteer projects give your program additional validity. You can keep track of the number of volunteers, their hours, and specific project statistics. At the end of the project, you can celebrate by giving the volunteers special recognition such as a small party or computer-generated bookmarks with the title of the project. By targeting these individuals, you give them additional encouragement and satisfaction.

VOLUNTEER MANAGER SATISFACTION

Establishing multiple evaluation criteria is a way to keep a balanced perspective on your program. By shifting away from one criterion (e.g., only counting the number of volunteers or the number of volunteer hours, etc.), you can help yourself and others appreciate and evaluate the impact of your program throughout the entire organization.

The Volunteer Program Evaluation (sample 9–2) can be used to evaluate your volunteer program. This form will help you gauge your program's successes.

I. Administrative Support	CURRENTLY HAPPENING	POSSIBLE IN FUTURE	IMPROBABLE AT THIS TIME
1. Paid volunteer manager position			
2. Program line item in budget			
3. Verbal support for volunteer training			
4. Financial support for volunteer training			
5. In-service training for volunteer supervision			
6. Recognition of program as part of public relations effort			
7. Centralized volunteer statistics			
8. Director writes articles about program			
9. Director comes to recognition events			
10. Budgeted funds for recognition awards			
11. Approval given for a volunteer handbook			
12. Office provided for volunteer manager			
13. Dollar value attached to a volunteer's time			
14. Volunteers recognized as unpaid staff			
15. Other_____			
II. Community/Recipient/Customer Support			
1. Verbal expression of thanks by recipient			
2. Written letters of thanks by recipient			
3. Outreach programs enhanced by volunteers			
4. Copies of "letters to the editor" about library volunteers			
5. Community recognition events include library volunteers			
6. Other_____			
III. Staff Support			
1. Staff willing to supervise volunteers			
2. Staff willing to be co-workers with volunteers			
3. Paid staff time available to train volunteers			
4. Paid time for staff supervising volunteers			
5. Staff identifies projects that won't get done without volunteers			
6. Staff can identify benefits of using volunteers			
7. Staff can define new volunteer opportunities and tasks			
8. Other_____			

IV. Volunteer Support	CURRENTLY HAPPENING	POSSIBLE IN FUTURE	IMPROBABLE AT THIS TIME
1. Assigned tasks meet personal interest and skill needs			
2. Assignments are interesting and challenging			
3. Volunteers are given opportunity to learn new tasks/skills			
4. Necessary supplies and equipment are provided			
5. Volunteer feels he or she is contributing to the library			
6. Volunteer feels she or he is contributing to the local community			
7. Volunteers are asked for their opinions			
8. Volunteers are assigned a contact person or supervisor			
9. Volunteers are introduced to staff			
10. Volunteers are given a tour of the facility			
11. Orientation training covers the needs of volunteers			
12. Task training is useful and adequate			
13. Volunteers feel they are part of the team			
14. The volunteer manager gives verbal recognition and feedback			
15. Staff members give verbal recognition and positive feedback			
16. Customers/recipients give verbal recognition and feedback			
17. Formal volunteer recognition events are held and well attended			
18. Adequate supervision is given to all volunteers			
19. There is a place to store personal effects			
20. There is a place to work on assigned tasks			
21. Volunteers are willing to train new volunteers			
22. Volunteers encourage others to become library volunteers			
23. Volunteers leave with a positive feeling of accomplishment			
24. Other_____			
V. Volunteer Manager Support			
1. Support is received from top administrators			
2. Support is received from immediate supervisor			
3. Support is received from peers			
4. Support is received from staff			
5. Support is received from volunteers			
6. Growth in number of library programs using volunteers			
7. Growth in number of volunteers			
8. Growth in number of volunteer hours			

(continued)

	CURRENTLY HAPPENING	POSSIBLE IN FUTURE	IMPROBABLE AT THIS TIME
9. Increase in volunteer diversity			
10. Increase in number of volunteers from recruitment efforts			
11. Increase in number of staff willing to supervise/work with volunteers			
12. Decline in number of failed volunteer efforts			
13. Decline in number of de-volunteered individuals			
14. Opportunity to share volunteer program information at manager meetings, in the community			
15. Volunteer training time built into staff schedules			
16. Staff and volunteers take responsibility for mutual problem-solving efforts			
17. Facility limitations on the use and number of volunteers are taken into account when looking at interlibrary comparisons			
18. Community demographics and lifestyle concerns are taken into account when looking at interlibrary comparisons			
19. Other_____			

Volunteer's name *(optional)*: _____

Job description: _____ Department _____

	POOR	FAIR	GOOD	EXCELLENT
To what extent did the description of your job represent what needed to be done?				
To what extent do you feel your job utilizes your talents and satisfies your reason for becoming a DPL volunteer?				
To what extent do you feel you are receiving support from your supervisor?				
Rate your relationships with team members:				
To what extent do you feel that the paid staff in this organization have acknowledged and appreciated your volunteer contribution?				

Things I have particularly enjoyed about being a library volunteer:

Suggestions for enhancing the program:

Additional comments:

3/2000

SECTION

10

Volunteer Motivation

What attracts individuals to seek volunteer opportunities with the library? What is their motivation? The answer to these questions can be as simple as the love of books or the desire to share the love of reading with others. What keeps volunteers coming back? They find the right fit. Their need to volunteer, their personalities, and their motivations match the opportunities and working environment in the library. To successfully recruit, it is important to understand the reason why people become volunteers. Your program will probably attract individuals with one or more of the following motivations:

- Opportunities to serve the community in a leadership capacity;
- Giving back to the community by helping others;
- Enriching family life;
- Time away from the demands of home and work;
- Acquiring or enhancing job skills; and
- Personal enrichment.

COMMUNITY LEADERSHIP

Individuals who feel the need to become active in government and make changes in the system can feel comfortable in a library setting. Their need to effect change can be satisfied if they work as a library trustee or board member. These individuals also may be adept at fund-raising or working as a link to the community to help sway the electorate in future decisions involving the library.

HELPING OTHERS

The desire to help others and give back to the community is a strong motivation that can be translated into volunteer work in the library. Homebound delivery of books, reading to children or seniors in nursing facilities or hospitals, helping with literacy programs, or working with customers to provide service at the online catalog or information desk are just a few of the jobs available to volunteers.

ENRICHING FAMILY LIFE

The library is a good place for families to volunteer. Examples of job opportunities include the delivery of books to individual homes or retirement communities, working together to present a story time, shelving books, or "adopting a shelf" in a favorite subject area. Children learn from example. Providing them with the opportunity to give to others and help build their community as a family encourages a self-image of serving and helping others in a learning environment. Volunteering can also develop a love of books, a desire for lifelong learning, and a respect for libraries. Providing these kinds of opportunities for families is good public relations for the library in the community, and helps to build a strong customer base for the future.

TIME AWAY FROM HOME AND WORK

A young mother can find some time away from her children and other responsibilities by volunteering for the library on nights or weekends when child care is available. Similarly, a caregiver for an elderly parent or individuals that work forty hours a week can volunteer at the library as a necessary break from their routine. Shelving, sorting, or working at an information desk can provide an outlet for meeting new friends and in some cases provide mental breaks from the demands of everyday life. The library can offer volunteer positions that do not require extensive training or time commitments. These are important considerations for individuals who want to volunteer but have family or work obligations.

ACQUIRING OR ENHANCING JOB-RELATED SKILLS

The Information Age and libraries are synonymous. Individuals wishing to learn more about computers, online database searching, or the World Wide Web can use the library as a way to gain more computer savvy. For individuals who are computer literate, assisting customers or staff is a good way to keep their skills current. Often the staff does not have enough time to spend with individual customers who need extra help or instruction. A capable volunteer can provide valuable assistance. Further, volunteers can hone their computer skills by working with word processing, spreadsheet, or database management packages in volunteer positions that use these skills.

PERSONAL ENRICHMENT

There are periods in life when people feel their discretionary time and activities are not providing a sense of personal fulfillment, challenge, or motivation. For these people, library volunteering affords a wide range of tasks and duties. Even the more mundane tasks, such as sorting books, can be beneficial as volunteers discover titles of books that appeal to them.

SECTION

11

Volunteer Needs Assessment

Before beginning the recruitment process, determine your library's need and the availability of volunteer work. One way to determine this need is to simply ask the staff through an interview process. Another approach is to develop a short questionnaire. The importance of a thorough needs assessment cannot be overlooked because it saves you time, improves the quality of the program, encourages staff participation, and fosters volunteer retention.

NEEDS ASSESSMENT QUESTIONNAIRE

In larger libraries, the needs assessment is determined on department, branch, or systemwide levels. The larger the library, the more formal the needs assessment must be to prevent any misunderstandings in your volunteer recruitment efforts.

A short questionnaire is designed to determine the need for volunteers. A set of questions (see sample 11-1) is sent with a cover letter to all department and branch managers to determine what they see as their current volunteer requirements. There may be some resistance to completing the form. Some managers may feel that by answering these questions, they are pointing out personal or departmental deficiencies or limiting their ability to get additional paid staff positions. For these or any other reasons you may have, it is wise for you to follow up with a telephone call to discuss their concerns.

A variation to the questionnaire is an e-mail survey that managers can respond to quickly and to which you can follow up at a later date.

Department: _____   Date: _____

1. What kinds of responsibilities do you have that can be delegated to free yourself for higher priority tasks?

   _____
   _____
   _____

2. What library services would you like to provide to the community that you cannot provide because of time commitments?

   _____
   _____
   _____

3. What library services would you like to provide to the community that you cannot because of the lack of individuals with specific skills or training?

   _____
   _____
   _____

4. What concerns or questions do you have about involving volunteers in your department?

   _____
   _____
   _____

5. What information would you need from the library administration before you would feel comfortable using volunteers?

   _____
   _____
   _____

6. What information would you need from the volunteer manager before you would feel comfortable using volunteers?

   _____
   _____
   _____

7. In what other areas or departments of the library do you think volunteers would be most effective?

   _____
   _____
   _____

Any other comments?

   _____
   _____
   _____
   _____
   _____
   _____

NEEDS ASSESSMENT INTERVIEWS

The needs assessment process can be introduced at a staff meeting where general questions and answers can be exchanged. The staff meeting can then be followed with small, informal interviews for gathering specific information.

A variation to this approach is to have the unit head invite key staff members to participate in the interview process. Managers and staff working together to determine the uses for volunteers in the department encourages a feeling of partnership and helps to solidify the volunteer program.

As you meet with each department, be sure that during this initial phase your questions are specific and directed toward the volunteer tasks. For example, find out how many volunteers are needed and if there is a workplace for each one. Also, is there a time of day that is better for training volunteers (such as the hour before the library opens) and how many volunteers can be trained at one time? What is the minimum number of hours needed per day, week, or month and how many shifts? Will supervising staff need to be present during the time the volunteers are working? What are the physical and educational requirements for each job? Do the jobs require a strong attention to detail when interruptions can lead to errors? Which jobs have completion dates, and which ones are continuous or sporadic? These are important questions that need answers.

The more information you have during the needs assessment period, the easier your recruitment and selection processes will be. Be flexible in your approach to each volunteer position. A manager may want a project done next week, but unless you have a volunteer already in mind, it may take you a week or longer to find the right person. During your discussions with the manager, you may want to negotiate volunteer work schedules and completion dates to give yourself enough leeway to recruit appropriate volunteers.

Once you have written your notes into a preliminary job description or a set of tasks, send a copy to the manager before you begin to recruit to make sure the information is correct and to clarify any gray areas.

12

Requisitioning Volunteers

Volunteer requisitioning is the process a department follows to request a volunteer with specific skills and aptitudes from the volunteer office. The process can be initiated informally by a conversation between the department head and volunteer manager or formally with the completion of a volunteer requisition form.

It is not unusual for a library manager to call you at the last minute to request a volunteer to help with a special project. If you try to respond quickly with a volunteer who is not capable of meeting departmental expectations, you can create negative feelings about using volunteers. Therefore, it is important to identify the requisition process as a separate part of recruitment because you are recognizing the need to clarify the specific kinds of volunteer skills that are required for a position. Therefore, if the need is to fill a well-established position that has a current and accurate job description, the requisitioning process is easy. In this case, there are expectations agreed upon by department managers, staff, and the volunteer manager about the type of volunteer and volunteer skills that will work best.

In an informal system, for example, the library manager would say to the volunteer manager, "Mary, our volunteer at the service desk will be moving out of state. We need to find a replacement." A recruitment announcement is written and posted in the library. In a formal system, a volunteer requisition form is completed and sent to the volunteer manager who proceeds with the recruitment process.

In either situation, the requisition process initiates the action to recruit. This process can be more problematic when there is a new volunteer position or an existing position with added duties. In each of these new situations, the job expectations will probably have to be renegotiated between you and the manager. Before you meet, it is important to write a tentative job description (or at least a list of job duties) to serve as a basis for discussion and to help all the parties focus on the position. Total agreement may not be possible, but it is only fair to any volunteer applicants that they are told, honestly, about the general expectations of the position at the beginning of the interview process. This is important for the future success of the volunteer experience.

In one case, a suburban library needed a volunteer to collate and staple a large supply of customer handouts. The workstation was in the copy room with a telephone that had six lines. One department manager thought it would be useful for the volunteer to answer the telephone during the extended monthly afternoon meetings. She was willing to write a short script to help the volunteer correctly answer the busy incoming lines. In the requisitioning process for this position, the mix of volunteer skills is very important. Some people might enjoy putting booklets together but do not have good telephone skills, or they may enjoy telephone work, but do not have the patience to make sure that the customer booklets are put together neatly and accurately. Therefore, if there is not clarification of the job requirements, then getting the right person for the position will be difficult. If the telephones are answered but the booklets do not get done, or the booklets are done but the telephone calls are poorly handled, the volunteer loses and this reflects on your skills as the volunteer manager.

KEY CLARIFICATION QUESTIONS IN THE REQUISITION PROCESS

Experienced volunteer managers develop key questions to ask a library manager or staff member when requisitioning a volunteer. The purpose of the questions is to verify what they want to happen (job description), when they want it to happen (time frame), where it will happen (location), and what type of volunteer they want to make it happen (qualifications).

Whether or not you decide to use a requisition form, making a follow-up call to the manager with focused questions can help you ensure the successful recruitment of the volunteer.

The following questions can be used to clarify the job requirements:

1. How soon do you need the project completed?

   ("I would like it done by the end of next week, but it definitely has to be completed by the first of the month.")

2. Where will the volunteer be working?

   ("I can put the volunteer in the back workroom, but that gets crowded or, better yet, I can use Sally's desk because she is on a three-month maternity leave.")

3. Can the volunteer flex hours or does the volunteer have to work when you are there?

   ("I need to be available to supervise the volunteer. I can do this only on Tuesday and Thursday afternoons, after 1:30 P.M.")

4. What type of individual are you most comfortable working with for this project?

   ("I don't want high school students because they are often too busy to come in regularly. I need someone who can follow instructions. I can work with a young mother who wants some volunteer hours or a retired senior who isn't doing a lot of traveling right now.")

5. When are you available to talk to the applicants?

   ("I can talk to them only when I'm off the reference desk on Tuesday and Thursday afternoons.")

In this example, you will need to find a volunteer who is willing to commit to completing the project and able to work in a situation of close supervision.

REQUISITION PROCEDURES

You will want to establish a set of requisition procedures. The following are suggestions:

1. A library manager or staff member will identify specific projects or special needs and submit a volunteer requisition form to the volunteer manager.
2. The volunteer manager will clarify the specific skill requirements and expectations of the position and review any pending volunteer applicants.
3. The volunteer manager is responsible for recruiting the appropriate volunteer.
4. The volunteer manager will collect volunteer applications, make initial contact, conduct screening interviews (telephone or in person), and make recommendations to the requesting staff manager.

USES FOR THE REQUISITION FORMS

Requisition forms can be used as part of the administrative process to:

1. Identify the number of staff needing volunteers;
2. Define the volunteer skill mix used by the library;
3. Document trends in the use of volunteers throughout the system;
4. Track the number of successful placements; and
5. Make needed changes and additions.

SECTION

13

Selling the Volunteer Program

Marketing is advertising your volunteer program to the community. It is letting people know what you are doing and what is available to them if they decide to volunteer their time. It is about going out to groups and speaking, or developing flyers and brochures and putting them in visible places to draw positive attention to who you are and what you are doing.

Recruitment, on the other hand, is an active plan to select volunteers for specific job opportunities.

MARKETING YOUR PROGRAM

Keep your program before the public eye. Advertise your need for volunteers, but don't forget to make the community aware of your program's accomplishments as well. Place articles in the local newspaper or library newsletter. Spotlight a volunteer of the month. Thank your volunteers by writing a letter to their employers with their permission. This shows their community spirit and highlights your program with local businesses. Display volunteer accomplishments in your library through pictures and plaques. Satisfied volunteers will recruit their friends and talk positively about your program in the community.

When possible, market your program by giving presentations to local organizations. You may find volunteers who are willing to talk about their work and what it's like to be a library volunteer.

DEVELOPING A RECRUITMENT CAMPAIGN

The following steps are necessary for an effective recruitment campaign:

1. Brainstorm a list of sources for potential volunteers;
2. Direct your recruitment campaign at these sources; and
3. Use your understanding of why people volunteer in your recruitment ads.

The staff has determined that there is a need for a storyteller in the children's department. They write up a request for a volunteer and you in turn write a job description. Decide on age group and key characteristics you will be looking for during the interview process. Then begin your recruitment campaign by brainstorming about all the resources you could use to advertise for your storyteller. If you are looking for a senior citizen, think of the local senior center, Retired Senior Volunteer Program (RSVP), or nearby churches, and then advertise according to the sources you

have listed. Include in your announcement key motivational phrases that would appeal to your recruitment pool such as: "encourage reading in young children" or " learn a new skill—the art of storytelling." Decide on the type of medium that would be most effective in attracting attention to your announcements. At the local senior center you can put up posters or advertise in the RSVP newsletter. You might want to recruit through your library's home page or through a local radio or cable station.

Do you want to diversify your volunteer pool? Send recruitment announcements to neighborhood newsletters or community centers. Contact local businesses or corporations to find out if they have an established employee volunteer program and advertise with them. Call local high schools or colleges. Many schools now require students to perform a minimum number of community service hours to graduate.

14

Recruitment of Volunteers

There are all types of library volunteers and this is an important fact to remember when putting together a specific program or filling a particular library need. Some managers make the mistake of trying to recruit people like themselves with the hidden assumption that these are the kinds of people most useful for the library. Others carry false stereotypes about people, which can hinder their recruiting efforts. As a volunteer manager, one of your most important tasks is to recruit different types of people to fill a variety of jobs.

For example, a volunteer who recently lost her husband after an extended illness needed a routine job that would get her out of the house. She was given the task of keeping the supplies straight, customer pencils sharpened, and scratch paper available near the public terminals. In other situations, a young man had the computer skills to update the library's home page, while a retired electrician had the interest, enthusiasm, and patience to help customers research their genealogy and read to groups of children during the morning story hour. When your aim is to recruit the best person for the job, library services are enhanced. However, the reverse is also true. If there is a poor match between a volunteer and the job, the outcome can be a deterioration of library services and staff-volunteer relationships.

Here is a breakdown of volunteers according to general categories:

Category	Examples
Age	children, young adults, adults, seniors
Gender	female, male
Interests	genealogy, literacy, archival, library support, and so forth

Category	Examples		Category	Examples
Skills, Training, and Education	technical, office, semiskilled, unskilled		Legal Distinctions	court-ordered, community
Time	ongoing, one-time project, special events		Disability	physical, visual, mental
Titles	volunteer intern, docent, friend, trustee			

These categories are *tools* to help you structure your recruiting efforts to target individuals who closely match the job requirements.

AGE

Young

Young volunteers often come from local service organizations, such as scouting, church groups, and school programs which require community service to graduate. For some, the library provides them with the opportunity to apply their knowledge of computers or online searching skills. For others, the library gives them a safe environment to complete their graduation requirements.

Adult

Adult volunteers can be recruited from local service and professional organizations as well as from companies that offer incentive programs for employees that perform community service. More recently, individuals with home-based businesses are volunteering as a way to reduce their feelings of isolation, just as parents with school-age children volunteer to get out of the house and meet other active adults.

In addition, workers who have been laid off from their jobs use volunteering to keep busy and to learn a new skill such as online searching while they continue to look for new employment.

Semiretired or recently retired individuals volunteer to help them transition from one lifestyle to another. The library provides a weekly structure to their lives and a new sense of community involvement.

GENDER

More library volunteers are female than male because traditionally the field of library science has been a female-dominated profession. However, the work is not gender-related (mending, reading to children, archival research, data entry, or data management). It can be done by anyone, but few men choose to donate their time.

Therefore, to successfully recruit men, it may be more effective to either identify specific, short-term tasks, projects, or events such as a fund-raising drive, or look at creating positions that some men might find more appealing in the area of technology or business.

INTERESTS

Recruiting special-interest volunteers requires a well-defined focus and perseverance. For example, one large urban library needed a volunteer to take care of their plants. A poster advertising the position was made for the library bulletin board, a public service announcement was placed in the local newspaper, and contacts were made with the garden clubs in the area. After three months there were still no prospects. Eventually, through word-of-mouth networking, a local resident, who raised flowers in her private greenhouse, volunteered. She not only took care of the plants, but also donated some from her greenhouse. In this case perseverance paid off.

Your goal is to match the "demonstrated" interests of a volunteer with the job requirements. An individual may never have read to seniors in a nursing home but has the interest and desire to try. Before you send her out alone, you might want to assign her to work with a volunteer already reading, so she can experience the task firsthand and gain the confidence to do the job herself or decide she doesn't really enjoy it. It is important to distinguish between interest and the talent or ability to do what is required. This is where your recruitment efforts and interviewing skills can help you identify an individual's "demonstrated" interests. This knowledge can be very important to the success of your program.

SKILLS, TRAINING, AND EDUCATION

Recruiting for specific skills or training or education is easier than recruiting for specific interests. For example, finding volunteers for jobs that require knowledge of computer graphics or desktop publishing requires people with specialized skills and knowledge. By phrasing your recruitment ads to reflect these skills or level of education, you limit the number of individuals qualified for the job. Then you can interview each of them, look at their portfolios, or ask for references to verify their skills and knowledge. This does not mean that the volunteer will automatically be successful in a library context, but at least you have laid the groundwork for future recruitment efforts.

TIME

For volunteers with busy schedules, short-term special projects or events are appealing. Working on these projects (e.g., a fund-raising campaign) allows them to concentrate on making the activity a top priority for that short period of time.

Special one-time projects or events also allow new volunteers to test the waters to see if they want to make a full-time commitment. Newcomers in town or individuals in life transitions can use special projects as a means to learn about the library and their community for a brief period of time.

There are volunteers who want a regular commitment. They want their week structured around ongoing activities. For these individuals, developing long-term friendships and having the regularity of a volunteer job are important intrinsic rewards.

The successful manager will recruit individuals based on their time and desire to volunteer. They will make sure their program includes long-term jobs and short-term projects.

TITLES

The number and type of volunteer positions depend on the size and structure of the library. At one end of the spectrum you can find community volunteers performing routine assigned tasks, and at the other end are the trustees (often overlooked as volunteers) setting library polices and standards. As the library organization grows, additional volunteer positions may evolve in the form of docents. These volunteers are usually separately identified, trained, and assigned specific kinds of tasks such as providing specialized customer service assistance or computer instruction.

Additionally there are the Library Friends groups in which volunteer members serve as a liaison to the community as well as helping the library through fund-raising efforts and special events or programs. The relationship between the library volunteers and the Friends group needs to be clarified, especially if there are individuals who volunteer in both organizations (see section 6).

LEGAL DISTINCTIONS

There are two distinct groups of volunteers found working in most libraries: (1) court-ordered (or court-appointed service; alternative service; or court-referred community service) and (2) community volunteers. The latter category is the largest group, and includes both youth and adults. The following discussion will center on court-ordered restitution.

Court-Ordered Restitution

Court-ordered restitution is the legally mandated sentence to perform community service in lieu of a jail term for a youth or adult who has been convicted of a minor offense. Most of these individuals are first-time offenders. Their misdemeanors may range from truancy, driving under the influence of drugs or alcohol, school fights, possession of drugs, driving infractions, or excessive parking tickets.

As the volunteer manager, you need to clarify with your administration, board, and staff your policies regarding which offenses will preclude individuals from volunteer activities. Many libraries will not accept anyone who has committed a burglary, robbery, has been charged with possession of a hidden weapon, or has demonstrated violent behavior. Others will not take individuals with drug offenses.

Remember the following three points: (1) you are not required to accept anyone the court refers to your library; (2) many of these individuals are talented and skilled people who made a mistake and want to work through the incident; and (3) you can terminate the individual whenever you deem it appropriate.

School principals also can assign community service hours to their students for minor infractions of the school rules. In one case, an elementary school principal assigned community service hours to a nine-year-old boy for throwing rocks at the building during recess. The child wanted to work at the library. The volunteer manager agreed if the parent remained in the library while the boy completed his assigned duties (sorting newspapers). This arrangement made it possible for the parent to share responsibility for the child's supervision.

DISABILITY

Individuals with physical or learning disabilities can be excellent library volunteers. It is essential that the staff is willing and the work appropriate to their skill levels. If they require extra supervision, will someone be provided? You are not obligated to find work for the disabled, but a good match can be rewarding.

A NOTE ON EDUCATION IN DIVERSITY

Diversity in the library is defined as working toward having a representation of volunteers from a cross-section of the population within your community. This means race, gender, and ethnic background but also age, physical and learning disabilities, beliefs, skill levels, and a wide array of educational levels (high school, college, graduate, and technical school). Review your volunteer pool and decide if it reflects your community. Are you reaching out to diverse populations through specialty newspapers? Are you placing announcements for volunteer opportunities throughout the community? Are you providing opportunities for the physically disabled? Review the current volunteer jobs to ensure that they vary in ability and school levels. If necessary, determine how you can make reasonable accommodations in the job tasks so that they are accessible to as many individuals as possible. Are there preconceived ideas about the jobs that limit volunteer diversity? If so, what in-service training can be provided to assist staff members to see the jobs and individuals differently? Diversity is an important part of the recruitment process.

DEFINITIONS OF VOLUNTEERS

The following definitions of volunteers can be used to clarify your recruiting efforts and are essential to include when writing policy statements.

> A library volunteer is anyone from the community who agrees to donate time, talent, and services.
>
> A library volunteer is an unpaid *staff member.*
>
> Library volunteers are diverse members of the community who share a common interest in helping the library.
>
> Library trustees are people elected or appointed to specific terms on the library governance board and are expected to initiate and affirm policy decisions for the library.
>
> Young adult volunteers are individuals who are at least sixteen years of age and can demonstrate maturity and reliability. They are capable of working with little or no supervision.
>
> Library youth volunteers are between the ages of twelve and fifteen. Projects are assigned to individuals or groups (such as the Scouts) when appropriate adult supervision is available.
>
> Library court-ordered volunteers are young adults or adults who are working at the library as restitution for offenses committed in the community.
>
> Friends of the Library are volunteers who hold dues-paying membership in a community group designed to help the library through fund-raising efforts and sponsoring or supporting special projects and events.

15

Recruitment Approaches

The most passive approach to recruitment is to wait for "walk-ins"— people who inquire at the circulation or reference desk about volunteer opportunities. Some libraries encourage citizen participation by having a special check-off box on their library card registration forms, or they list opportunities and contact information on their Internet home page.

As your volunteer program grows, specific types of skills are often required either by the department or job specifications. If you are lucky, the right volunteers will "walk in" at the appropriate time. In most cases you will probably have to actively recruit someone from the community. The following are suggestions for successful, low-cost ways to attract volunteers.

ACTIVE RECRUITMENT

Networking

Both current volunteers and staff know someone with the skill, talent, and interest to fill a specific volunteer position. By talking to these people, you can extend your network and increase your chances of finding the appropriate volunteer for the job.

Individuals can also be recruited through word-of-mouth advertising. For example, a volunteer enjoys her work and talks about it to friends and family. Her enthusiasm encourages others to explore similar opportunities with your library.

Flip Charts, Posters, and Flyers

You can make a flip chart or multicolored poster to identify current volunteer jobs. Post them by the main entrance, and you have an effective way of attracting attention to available positions.

Bulletin boards located throughout the community are very good places to advertise your volunteer positions. This approach is another way to attract a large, diverse number of interested people.

Flyers take time to design, reproduce, and distribute. However, they are an excellent way to recruit volunteers and advertise your program. Flyers are versatile. They can be distributed in a variety of ways such as by placing them on desks or posting them on bulletin boards (see sample 15-1).

The World Wide Web

Currently, many libraries are developing their own home pages on the Internet. An increasing

SAMPLE 15-1
Be a Homebound Volunteer Flyer

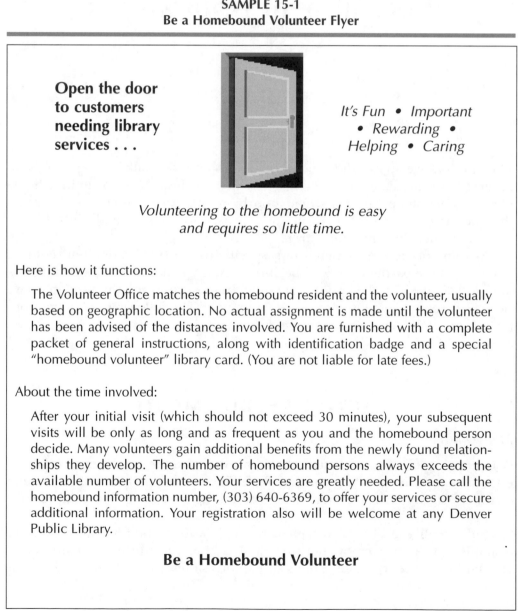

Open the door to customers needing library services . . .

It's Fun • Important • Rewarding • Helping • Caring

Volunteering to the homebound is easy and requires so little time.

Here is how it functions:

The Volunteer Office matches the homebound resident and the volunteer, usually based on geographic location. No actual assignment is made until the volunteer has been advised of the distances involved. You are furnished with a complete packet of general instructions, along with identification badge and a special "homebound volunteer" library card. (You are not liable for late fees.)

About the time involved:

After your initial visit (which should not exceed 30 minutes), your subsequent visits will be only as long and as frequent as you and the homebound person decide. Many volunteers gain additional benefits from the newly found relationships they develop. The number of homebound persons always exceeds the available number of volunteers. Your services are greatly needed. Please call the homebound information number, (303) 640-6369, to offer your services or secure additional information. Your registration also will be welcome at any Denver Public Library.

Be a Homebound Volunteer

number are also listing their volunteer opportunities. Online recruiting is an excellent way to contact people who are already library users and familiar with computers.

In addition, many towns and cities have home pages. Many of these list agencies and community groups that use volunteers. Find out if your community has one and make sure your opportunities are listed.

Group Presentations

An invitation to speak or give presentations to local groups can also serve as a means to recruit volunteers and advertise your program. Remember your enthusiasm for volunteerism is more important than your formal public speaking skills.

Public Service Announcements, Newspapers, and Newsletters

Radio stations and local access television will take public service announcements. It is important to work with a knowledgeable station representative to make sure you include all the appropriate information for this medium.

Large metropolitan dailies and small suburban or community weekly newspapers will usually run your announcements as a community service (check to see if they already regularly list community and volunteer activities). If you contact the editor first for specific information on submitting articles or announcements, you can save yourself a lot of time.

Don't forget to include the specialty newspapers in your area. These may help you recruit a volunteer with a skill or talent you need to complete a job. For example, local sports photographs are donated to a library. They need to be identified and cataloged. You might want a volunteer

with an interest in sports to work on the project. First, research the local print media to see if there is a newspaper dealing with community sports. Then write an advertisement emphasizing the need for a volunteer interested in a short-term project to identify and categorize photographs of community sports events. Remember to take into consideration the newspaper publication schedule and make sure your ad coincides with their time frame and your need for the volunteer. Basically, it is this easy to recruit from a newspaper.

Many local organizations have newsletters such as school PTAs, homeowner associations, civic groups, garden, hobby, or travel clubs, and other community interest groups. The reference desk and Chamber of Commerce can provide you with a list of names and key contacts. The process you use is very similar to placing an ad in the local newspaper.

Volunteer Referral Organizations and Networks

In larger cities there are nonprofit groups (e.g., United Way) who use volunteers and also refer them to other organizations. Make sure your program is listed with these agencies. Usually these organizations do very little screening before making a referral, so write a thorough job description and plan to interview all prospective volunteers.

Volunteer Fairs

Some communities organize a volunteer fair for nonprofit groups on an annual basis. It is certainly advantageous to attend one of these fairs and distribute literature about your program. In addition, it is good publicity for you and the library.

DEVELOPING A RECRUITMENT CAMPAIGN

Following is an example of the process to recruit a storyteller for your library:

The staff has determined there is a need for a storyteller in the children's department. They

write a request for a volunteer and you in turn write a job description. First, you need to decide what age group the storyteller will address and key characteristics you need based on the job requirements. Then you can begin the recruitment campaign by listing all the resources you can use to advertise for the storyteller. If you are looking for a senior citizen, think about recruiting from the local senior center, RSVP, or nearby churches, and include a list of newspapers or newsletters they might read. Your announcement needs to include key motivational phrases that appeal to your recruitment pool, such as "encourage reading in young children" or "learn a new skill—the art of storytelling." Then you need to decide on the type of recruitment method that would be effective in attracting attention to your announcements. At the local senior center, you can put up posters or advertise in the RSVP newsletter. You might want to recruit through your library's home page or through a local access radio or cable station.

Do you want to diversify your volunteer pool? Send recruitment announcements to neighborhood newsletters or community centers. Also, contact local businesses or corporations to find out if they have an established employee volunteer program and advertise with them. Call the local high schools or colleges; many now require students to perform a minimum number of community service hours to graduate.

16

Volunteer Application Form

The volunteer application form is an important, multipurpose tool. It serves to let potential volunteers know that there is a process that matches their skills and experience with your library requirements. A well-done application allows you to conduct a better recruiting interview because you can use the application to discuss prior work and volunteer experiences and explore areas of interests that relate to library needs. Most importantly, it allows you to screen individuals who do not meet the job requirements. Finally, application forms can be used to collect volunteer statistics. You can tabulate the number of applications received versus the number of volunteers accepted and determine which recruitment approaches work best for which type of volunteer positions.

Your application form can be either simple or complex depending on the information you need to gather to satisfy any library administration requirements. It is possible for volunteer applications to ask more specific personal questions than an employee form because the latter must comply with the requirements of federal and state employment laws. Each library system will differ on the type of questions to include on the form, so be sure to get your application reviewed and approved before using it.

As you begin the process of developing an application form, important questions to ask your supervisor are:

Who gives final review to the volunteer application form(s)?

Can there be two forms, one for general community volunteers and one for court-referred volunteers?

Can a simplified version of the form be used for youth volunteers if necessary?

KEY COMPONENTS
OF AN APPLICATION FORM

The following are some key elements of a volunteer application form.

NAME AND CONTACT INFORMATION

1. Address including zip code
2. Current telephone and pager number (Note: It is important to make sure that the volunteer keeps you informed of any changes in the contact information)
3. Social security number (optional but if the volunteer position requires a background check, you need to have this information)
4. Driver's license number (optional unless the position includes driving, such as delivering or picking up books. You will need this to get a copy of the Motor Vehicle Record (MVR) from your state driver's license bureau to check the applicant's driving history for tickets and accidents.)

TIME COMMITMENTS

Use a checklist or short answer section to find out when the applicant will be available (i.e., times and days during the week) as well as the number of volunteer hours per week.

SKILLS AND EXPERIENCES

Use a checklist of specific skills that can be based on work or volunteer experience, avocation, or talents. The indicated skills can be matched to library requirements for specific jobs. This list can be expanded to include a self-rating level of competency for each skill area. If you have a skill-based test related to the volunteer position, use it to determine whether or not to train or reject the applicant.

INTEREST AREAS

Use a checklist or a place for applicants to write about their interest areas (not demonstrated skills). For instance, an individual has not read to children's groups before but would be interested in trying it out.

LOCATION PREFERENCE

If you have more than one library in your system, it is a good idea to let the volunteer indicate which library is the preferred one for volunteering. Some applicants may want to stay close to their home and others are open to volunteering where ever there is need.

REASONS FOR VOLUNTEERING

A simple checklist of reasons for volunteering can help you to open the discussion and relax the individual during the interview process. It can also serve to clarify the reasons for volunteering and eliminate individuals who find they are really not interested in library work.

EDUCATION LEVEL

You can use a checklist or fill-in-the-blank to find out the highest grade completed, major area of study, and any additional training courses. This information can be used to place applicants. Libraries are staffed with a high percentage of college-educated individuals. Many have advanced degrees. Mature volunteers may not have the educational level of some of the current staff members, but they have life experience and on-the-job training that will certainly enrich and diversify library services.

GENDER (OPTIONAL)

During the interview process you can identify the applicant's gender. Except in rare cases, gender information on the application form is primarily a source of statistical information for future reports to the administration or for fund-raising purposes.

AGE CATEGORIES (OPTIONAL)

Broad age categories on the application can give you an idea of the types of volunteers interested and the kinds of assignments that are attracting them. Age categories are also a source of statistical information that can help you later in your recruitment efforts.

PHYSICAL LIMITATIONS

If the applicant has any physical limitations that would restrict performing the job it is important to know for risk management as well as for job placement.

EMERGENCY CONTACT INFORMATION

It is important to include a space for the name and number of an emergency contact.

REFERENCES

You need to ask for references who know the applicant in a volunteer role (if possible; some applicants have never volunteered). References can include people who know the individual through membership in a professional, service, civic, or religious organization because these are usually voluntary groups. It is often easier to conduct reference checks with these organizations than with larger companies or public agencies.

CONTRACTUAL STATEMENT

A signed and dated statement on your application form should indicate that the applicant realizes that the tasks are assigned on the basis of library needs and requirements. Furthermore, if the assigned tasks are not done to library standards, the volunteer relationship can be terminated. The contractual agreement implies that the library takes volunteering seriously and the volunteer agrees to follow all library requirements (see samples 16-1, 16-2, 16-3, and 16-4).

Please return this application to: Volunteer Coordinator's Office
East Library and Information Center   5550 N. Union Blvd.   Colorado Springs, CO 80918
(719) 531-6333, x1251   http://library.ppld.org

Name _____ Date _____

Address _____

City _____ State _____ Zip _____

Home phone _____ Work phone _____ CO Drivers Lic. No._____

Library Location Preference *(check all that apply)*

☐ Cheyenne Mountain   ☐ Monument   ☐ Penrose   ☐ Sand Creek
☐ East Library   ☐ Old Colorado City ☐ Rockrimmon   ☐ Ute Pass
☐ Fountain   ☐ Palmer Lake   ☐ Ruth Holley   ☐ Bookmobile

Availability *(circle all that apply)*   Mon. Tues. Weds. Thurs. Fri. Sat. Sun.   Time available_____

Work Experience *(include volunteer and military service)*

1. Last or present position
   Employer_____ City and State_____
2. Previous position
   Employer_____ City and State_____

Education *(check highest level)*

☐ Elementary   ☐ High School   ☐ Technical School   ☐ Some College
☐ College degree or professional training in_____

Personal References *(Give two references, preferably from the local community, who are not your present employer or a relative).*

	Name	Daytime phone #	Relationship
1.			
2.			

I certify that the answers contained in this application are true and complete to the best of my knowledge. My volunteer service is conditional upon completion of the application and verification of the references found on this application. I am offering my services as a volunteer. If my offer is accepted, I will not be entitled to compensation for any services I provide.

Signature_____ Date_____

Parental Permission

If you are under 16, please have a parent/legal guardian sign the following permission form:

I (print) _____ parent/legal guardian, grant permission

for (print) _____ to volunteer at the Pikes Peak Library District.

Parent/Legal Guardian Signature:_____ Date:_____

VOLUNTEER SKILL/INTEREST INVENTORY

Indicate those areas of skill/interest that pertain to you.
Mark as many as are applicable.

Adult Literacy Program

_____ Right to Read (adult literacy)

Arts/Graphics/Crafts

_____ Art design
_____ Art exhibits/fairs
_____ Calligraphy
_____ Crafts
_____ Cartooning
_____ Displays/bulletin boards
_____ Graphics
_____ Photography/video

Clerical/Office Work

_____ Answering phones
_____ Clerical/office work
_____ Filing
_____ Photocopying
_____ Record keeping
_____ Telephoning

Communications/Information

_____ Brochure/newsletter
_____ Editing
_____ Public speaking
_____ Video/films
_____ Writing

Program Support

_____ Book discussion group leader
_____ Clown/mime/juggler
_____ Drama/theater arts
_____ Exotic animals
_____ Music
      Type:_____
      Instrument(s):_____
_____ Organize special events
_____ Present educational program
      Topic (s): _____
_____ Puppeteering
_____ Storytelling
_____ Travel experience

General Library Work

_____ Book mending
_____ Shelving books
_____ Adopt-a-Shelf (shelfreading)

Library Research

_____ Archives/manuscripts
_____ Creating book lists
_____ Genealogy
_____ Local history
_____ Opinion surveys/polling
_____ Oral history

Hobbies/Interests

_____ Baking
_____ Carpentry
_____ Indoor plant care
_____ Handyman skills
_____ Outdoor plant care
_____ Sewing
_____ Upholstery
_____ Other
      Type: _____

Outreach Services

_____ Book sales
_____ Book store
_____ Delivering books to shut-ins
_____ Reading to children
_____ Reading to seniors

Computer Skills

_____ Database searches
_____ Data entry
_____ Desktop publishing
_____ Spreadsheet experience
_____ Word processing
Describe software you are familiar
with: _____
_____
_____

(continued)

VOLUNTEER PLACEMENT
For Office Use Only

Name _____

Reports to _____ Branch location _____

Start date _____ Postion _____

Type of Volunteer Position *(check one)*

☐ Regular ☐ Right to Read ☐ School credit ☐ Court-ordered ☐ YAC

☐ Project (project name) _____

Personal Information

Birth date _____ (mo/day) SSN_____ - _____ - _____

Marital Status ☐ Single ☐ Married Sex ☐ M ☐ F

Race *(optional)* ☐ Black ☐ Hispanic ☐ Am. Indian ☐ Asian ☐ White

Emergency contact person _____ Relationship _____

Home address _____ City_____State _____

Home phone _____ Work phone _____

Attached *(check if completed)*

Volunteer agreement form signed _____ Name tag issued _____

Volunteer Not Placed

Brief description why _____

_____

_____

Separation

Date _____ Reason _____

_____

_____

Recommendation to Rehire ☐ Yes ☐ No

City of Aurora Library & Recreation Services
www.ci.aurora.co.us

Name _____   Birthday (month/day) _____

Address _____

City _____

State and zip code _____

Telephone   (H) _____

             (W) _____

E-mail _____

Occupation _____

Languages you speak fluently _____   Languages you read fluently _____

Skill/talents *(please describe)* _____

Experience with children *(please describe)* _____

Are you interested in storytelling? ☐   Reading stories? ☐   Both? ☐

Emergency contact
Name _____
Phone _____

Availability

Days *(please circle all that apply)*   M   T   W   Th   F

Times   Mornings _____

          Afternoons _____

How often are you available to read?   Weekly? ☐   Once a Month? ☐   Please be specific: _____

Can you make a one-year commitment?   Yes ☐   No ☐

Are there two people you know well, either professionally or personally, who can talk about your ability or experience in working with children?

Name: _____   Phone # _____

Name: _____   Phone # _____

The safety of children in this program is the first concern of the library. We require every prospective volunteer to pass a police background check. Please complete the attached form and return it with your application.

I have read the job description and guidelines and understand the responsibilities and duties of this position.

Signature of Applicant _____   Date: _____

Signature of Parent/Guardian if under 18 _____   Date: _____

Douglas
Public Library District

D   P   L   D

Last Name _____ First _____ Telephone (home) _____

Street Address_____ City_____Zip Code_____Telephone (work) _____

Age Categories

___ under 16
___ 16 - 18
___ 19 - 24
___ 25 - 39
___ 40 - 54
___ over 55

Education

Highest level completed
___ Grammar School
___ High School
___ Technical School
___ Some College
___ College degree in
_____
___ Professional training in
_____

Availability

Monday   _____
Tuesday   _____
Wednesday   _____
Thursday   _____
Friday   _____
Saturday   _____
Sunday   _____

Facility Preference

___ Highlands Ranch Library, Highlands Ranch
___ Lone Tree Library, Lone Tree
___ Parker Library, Parker
___ Philip S. Miller Library, Castle Rock
___ Anywhere needed

_____ Total hours needed?
_____ Completion deadline?
_____ Which court system?

Please describe why the court ordered community service hours

_____

In case of an emergency contact _____
(NAME & PHONE)

Do you have any physical limitations restricting your activities? _____ Yes _____ No   If yes, please explain:

_____

Is there any medical information that you wish to share that
would be helpful for the staff to know for a medical emergency_____

I understand that, as a court ordered community service worker, I will be assigned to perform whatever duties the library considers most necessary and helpful to its operation. I also understand that
my work will be reviewed and, at any time, the library may terminate my services.

Signature: _____   Date: _____

Complete the skills / interest inventory on the back, sign both this application and the agreement
form and return them to your local library or mail them to:

Volunteer Services Department, Douglas Public Library District, 961 S. Plum Creek Blvd.,
Castle Rock, CO 80104. Phone: 303-688-8752   Fax: 303-688-1942

Indicate those areas of skill/interest which pertain to you.
Mark as many as are applicable.

____ art design	____ displays/bulletin boards	**Computer Skills**
____ crafts	____ clerical/office work	____ data entry
____ cartooning	____ outdoor plant care	____ desktop publishing
____ filing	____ indoor plant care	____ word processing
____ baking	____ carpentry skills	____ spreadsheets
____ photocopying	____ used book sales	____ database searching
____ shelving books	____ handyman skills	
____ painting	____ sewing skills	

As a court-ordered community service worker with the Douglas Public Library District I agree to the following guidelines:

The library agrees:

1. To provide you with a safe work environment.
2. To provide supervision and training by a member of the library staff, who will answer your questions and provide feedback regarding your work.

As a court-ordered community service worker, I agree:

1. To accept the guidance and decisions of the staff.
2. To recognize the function of the paid staff and stay within the bounds of a community service worker's responsibilities.
3. To always wear a volunteer badge. (They are kept in the file box with the time cards.)
4. To report on time, as scheduled, and check in with the supervisor or staff upon arrival. Failure to do so can result in termination.
5. To fill out and have a staff member sign my time card each shift I work.
6. To inform my supervisor as soon as possible if I am unable to keep my schedule.
7. To notify my supervisor and the volunteer department if I do not intend to complete my hours at the library.
8. To dress appropriately and act courteously to patrons and employees. (The library is a public place where attitude and appearance are important. Things need to be done accurately.)
9. To maintain the dignity and integrity of the library with the public and patron confidentiality, which is guaranteed under Colorado law. I will not discuss any patrons by name or their reading selections outside of the library.
10. I understand that upon completion of my hours, it is my responsibility to see that my final time card is sent to the Volunteer Services Department. The Volunteer Services Department requires seven days to process your confirmation papers after receiving your final time card. Your signed papers will arrive via the postal service unless special arrangements have previously been made.

_____   _____
Court-Ordered Worker's Signature   Staff's Signature

17

Interviewing and Selection

Interviewing is a focused conversation designed to elicit responses that help you make a decision about inviting an individual to become a volunteer with the library. From your initial introduction to your final departing comments, you are representing the library and setting the tone for any future relationships. If you are new to conducting interviews, you may find it difficult to adopt a relaxed, conversational style. This is not as important as making sure you focus on the skills and qualities needed for the volunteer position because losing your focus here can result in an individual being improperly selected for the job. Think of the interview as a focused conversation that is semiscripted, both in your words and behavior. Your personal script needs to concentrate on specific points of information to give and questions to ask the individual sitting across from you.

TYPES OF INTERVIEWS

There are primarily two types of interviewing techniques: telephone and face-to-face interviewing. Telephone interviewing is useful to screen out potential volunteers who may not have the kind of library interests, time commitment, or motivation to do the work. It can also encourage individuals to come in for further information and at the same time create enthusiasm for the available job and your library.

Face-to-face interviews are used to make either a final decision about hiring a volunteer or, more commonly, to screen volunteers for a staff member position as the first step in a two-step process, with the library manager making the final decision. Both of these interviewing functions are important to the total process of finding the right volunteer for the position.

When you screen a potential volunteer, your task is to find the kind of volunteer who will fit the departmental subculture and management style of the staff member in charge. A loud, fast-talking, highly animated individual is not likely to work out well with a department managed by a quiet, deliberate, and soft-spoken library supervisor, regardless of the volunteer's skill level.

Your conversation ending the interview can be: (1) "yes, you have just the skills and interests we are looking for and we would like you to begin on Wednesday," (2) a polite "thank you for coming in, but at present there is no match between our library volunteer requirements and your skills," or (3) "you have the volunteer background and skills we would like to have, but at the moment there are no openings and I would like to keep you on my calling list so I can place you in one of our future openings." Be honest with each applicant.

VOLUNTEER SELECTION

In unique instances, more than one capable volunteer passes the screening process. Each is eligible for consideration but only one position is available. If you cannot expand the volunteer hours or offer alternative volunteer tasks, then it is very important that the selection process be based on specified selection criteria. The criteria may be the number of weekly hours, scheduled availability, time-off requests, skill mix, the ability to handle task demands, or fitting into the organizational culture. The latter criterion is less specific, but just as important.

At the selection stage, job descriptions, task cards, or actually demonstrating what is expected of the volunteer can make the decision easier. Be honest, realistic, and upfront about the expected duties. This candor is not only fair to the volunteer, but it allows her time to reexamine her decision and decide if this is truly the job she wants to do at your library. For example, a position opens up mending books and the supervisor is willing to train no more than two people to do the work. Three capable people want the job. The selection process is made easier if you have a list of criteria that you can use to eliminate one of the three people. You can then offer another available job to the third person with the promise that she will be the first considered if a mending position opens up.

After offering a position to the potential volunteer, allow her to think about the work overnight or set a follow-up date to meet with her and discuss the tasks more fully. After talking about the library opportunity with family members, she may find that the scheduling demands will not work out or that this is not quite what she had in mind when she decided to volunteer at the library. A good interview will lead to a self-selection process in which the potential volunteer opts out, wishes to do something else, or comes back very excited.

An important part of the interviewing process is to find out what the volunteer likes to do or wants to avoid. Some people do not like to make telephone calls while others avoid a lot of people contact. It is important not to oversell a position to a marginal volunteer just to get someone to do the job. A bad fit between the volunteer and the position will likely leave negative feelings among staff, managers, other volunteers, and the misplaced volunteer.

Few people enjoy being rejected, especially for volunteer positions, yet using good interviewing skills may lead you to such a decision. In structuring the interview questions, you can assist unqualified people to self-select out. If this does not happen, then you have to "reject" the volunteer for the position.

Inherent in the general process of volunteer interviewing, selecting, and rejecting is the library's public relations function. In turning down people due to lack of skills, interests, attitudes, personal schedules, or "fit" with the library organization, it is essential to recognize that these people are probably customers and tax-paying citizens. A positive rejection may do little or no harm, but a negative one can generate intense, nasty comments about the library in general or you as the volunteer manager.

Ideally, you want to match the volunteer to another position, which converts the rejection into a new library opportunity. If this is not possible, you may choose to suggest that she explore other community groups that use volunteers or refer her to a counterpart in a community organization. In this instance, a rejection can lead to another contact name. If you feel a referral is inappropriate or by library policy it is not allowed, then you will have to reject the individual as politely as possible.

Scripting

New interviewers fumble for words. Experienced interviewers use a variety of personal scripts to keep the conversation focused, mutually useful, informative, and friendly.

Depending on your library administration, you may be required to follow strict hiring guidelines that include not asking illegal questions on race, religious affiliation, national origin, sex, age, disability, marital status, childbearing plans, or arrest record. Your human resources manager will likely have a list of not-to-be-asked questions or the reference department can locate a copy for you.

Since employment affirmative action laws do not directly cover volunteers, your administration may not care what questions you ask potential volunteers. For this reason, you have more leeway to ask a wider range of questions. However, in most cases there is little need to ask questions in the interview that touch on any of the above topics. Whether one is married, divorced, legally separated, or living with someone has no bearing on how well they can answer library telephones, reshelve books, or clip materials for pamphlet files.

Preparing Scripts

When scripting you need to include five kinds of questions:

1. Background;
2. Skill based;

3. Time and schedule;
4. Attitude/culture; and
5. Probing questions.

The first set of questions is designed to meet the specific skill requirements of the position. If the task requires finger dexterity, as in book mending, you can ask about the types of paid and unpaid positions a person has held that required the use of his or her hands, or about hobbies and recreational activities that involve finger dexterity. Anyone who knits, makes porcelain statues, or repairs their own household furniture demonstrates the skills necessary for mending. However, this does not mean they can do mending or even want to, but it certainly shows the capability to do this job or similar tasks.

Interviews for a volunteer job that requires public contact, such as calling to let customers know their reserved items are available or assisting at the circulation counter, can be scripted with questions about current or former paid or unpaid positions that required contact with customers. You could ask the interviewee whether, if she had to contact a stranger, she would prefer to write a letter or call on the telephone and why? People who do not like to talk to strangers may prefer to write a letter and wait for a response. Someone more comfortable talking to strangers might also be at ease calling customers on the telephone.

Time and schedule questions are important to ask to reduce potential conflicts or misunderstandings later on. If the individual has travel plans, as many retired or semiretired persons do, you need to be honest about library expectations. If a potential volunteer has three-month travel plans, let her know that you will be glad to work with her when she returns.

Some library volunteer tasks are fluid and can be adjusted to a person's schedule. Other tasks have to be performed at certain times of the day, week, or month, or when a particular staff member is present in the library and can supervise the volunteer. A question you can ask is, "Which days and times of the week will best fit your schedule to volunteer?" The answer can be compared with what the library needs or you can identify where scheduling adjustments need to be made.

Questions on attitudes and organizational culture cover the "soft skills" a person has in relating and working with others in a library setting. Even in a relaxed interview situation, there is a formality that can camouflage how an individual may actually work with other volunteers and staff members. Scripting questions here attempts to get at a person's temperament (intense or easygoing), expectations about others (demanding, supportive, or participative), outlook on life (optimistic or pessimistic), disposition (sense of humor or humorless), and motive(s) for volunteering in a public library. You can use questions such as: "What is your reaction when a project you are working on goes wrong and you have to redo the work? When someone accuses you of making an error, which you did not do, how do you handle the situation? When you have a bad day, what do you do to cheer yourself up?" A good response to each of these questions would be to demonstrate a positive attitude.

Probing questions allow you to ask more in-depth questions following any initial answer that is given to you. Poor interviewers often take the first answer they hear without asking a follow-up or probing question to obtain more information. A volunteer applicant may give quick responses to your questions because she is nervous. If you take these at face value, you may be disappointed later on. Learn to use probes. Two easy to use nonverbal probes are: (1) wait out pauses and let the person speak further on the topic; and (2) give a slight positive nod of your head and simultaneously make eye contact. This allows the applicant time to continue.

As in any good conversation, there is a give and take in the flow of words, but you should limit your side of the dialogue to about 25 percent talking and 75 percent active listening.

Remember to listen for behavioral and attitudinal examples that will give you a clue to the type of person applying for volunteer work. If you must reject the candidate for any reason, have an alternative script prepared. A firm voice can be used to state "You and I have discussed our volunteer program and I do not see a fit between your skills and our current library requirements. I think your desire to do community volunteering is commendable. Our reference department has a list of local community organizations that use volunteers and I'll be glad to direct you to one of our librarians. Thank you for thinking about the library." In the behavioral part of your script, you are standing up and moving the person toward the door.

A sample list of interview questions is included here (see sample 17-1). The questions are broken down into five categories. With experience you can learn to blend and script these five types of questions into your interviews.

SAMPLE 17-1
Sample Interview Questions

Focused Background Questions

1. What types of work or community experiences have you had that would make you a good library volunteer?
2. What is it about libraries that makes you want to volunteer here?
3. Have you used our library services? Which one(s)?
4. What type of reading materials do you enjoy?
5. When you are in a library, where do you usually go first? Second?
6. What kinds of jobs have you observed in the library that most excite you?
7. What personal issues might interfere with your volunteer duties?

(continued)

Skill-Based Questions

8. What are the top three skills or talents that you would bring to our library?

9. Are there any skills you are trying to improve?

10. Have you taken any recent workshops or classes? What "lifelong" learning experiences can you bring to the job?

11. Describe your computer experience at work or at home?

12. Some of our volunteer jobs require precise work and others are more general. Which type of work would you feel more comfortable doing if we had both positions open?

13. What types of paid or volunteer jobs or tasks do you like to do the most?

14. What type of paid or volunteer jobs or tasks do you least like to do?

15. What was your most challenging volunteer or work task?

16. If you could design your ideal volunteer job for the library, what would it be like?

17. If your are assigned to a job that requires us to have a copy of your driving record or a police background check on file, what would these records show?

Time and Schedule Questions

18. Which days of the week are the best for you?

19. What times of day are best for you?

20. How long per day can you volunteer for us?

21. What time of day do you do your best work?

22. Are there any times of day or days in the week that are definitely out for doing volunteer work?

23. Do you have any foreseeable scheduling problems if you started with us next week?

24. When can you start?

Attitude and Organizational Culture Questions

25. What prompts you to want to volunteer at our library?

26. What kinds of organizations or groups have you worked or volunteered for that are most like a library?

27. What kinds of volunteer work have you done over the past five years?

28. In what type of settings do you enjoy doing volunteer work?

29. If you could choose the kinds of people you would work with, what would they be like?

30. When you wake up in the morning, what kinds of activities get you going?

31. What do you do for relaxation, personal pleasure, or fun?

32. When you have a problem with a task, do you ask someone for help or try to figure it out yourself?

33. If I were to call your references, what type of comments about your strengths and areas of improvement might they comment on?

Probing Questions

34. Why?
35. What do you mean?
36. When did that happen?
37. How?
38. Where?
39. Tell me more.
40. Can you please expand on that point for me?
41. I am not sure that I understand.
42. How do you think that experience might relate to our library?
43. Are there any problems that might interfere with your volunteer duties?
44. Paraphrase her answer, then ask: "Is this what you mean?"

SECTION

18

Reference Requests

There are certain volunteer jobs that require more than an interview. Any work involving vulnerable customers (e.g., children), at-risk individuals (homebound customers), or the handling of sensitive or confidential customer information needs to be closely monitored. Today, a public institution or nonprofit agency must be careful to make sure they hire responsible individuals with a past record of honesty and integrity. The bottom line is that background and personal reference checks protect you and the library as well as the volunteer and library customers from potential problems.

BACKGROUND CHECKS

Before you initiate or reevaluate current services that require more information from the volunteer, talk to the library attorney or the city or county legal department. Make sure that you and the library administration have a basic understanding of the state's statutes on offenses against individuals. The law can act as a guide to help you write the volunteer policy on this issue. For example, the types of offenses that can preclude acceptance for a volunteer position can include but not be limited to the following types of convictions: crimes against children, driving while under the influence of drugs, substance abuse, sexual abuse, elderly abuse, domestic violence, fraud, and theft.

Background checks must be done with the consent of the individual. Make sure you check with the police to find out what personal and demographic information is necessary to complete a background check. The local police or a large volunteer agency may already have the information form or a generic release statement that you can use or modify for library use.

At some point you may have a situation that cannot be written in your volunteer policy statement but needs to be considered; for example, when a background check suggests the possibility of irresponsible behavior, a violent nature, or unsafe habits. What if an individual applies for a position in homebound services, you send in a request for a background check, and the report comes back with an arrest but no conviction for domestic violence? What are your options and how can this situation be addressed? At this point you need to require more information and clarification from the individual concerning the arrest. Keep the discussion confidential and always keep detailed records. You may want to seek administrative or legal counsel before deciding to use this individual as a volunteer.

There are several levels of background checks. The most basic is a name and social security search. This provides statewide information on whether the individual has a police record. A more thorough check requires a fingerprint. This provides a more accurate and detailed report including information on whether the individual is going by an assumed name. The third and fourth levels, respectively, include an FBI report that is authorized during criminal investigations and finally an international search through Interpol records, neither of which public libraries will probably use.

Keep in mind that there is a graduated fee when requesting background information. In addition and most importantly, the physical report must be kept in the strictest confidence and in a secure location. Information leaked from these reports may result in a lawsuit.

PERSONAL REFERENCE CHECKS

Calling a volunteer's references helps you to learn more about the personality of the individual and how he or she relates to other people. Keep your questions specific to the job. Explain the reason for your call, something about the job, and ask how they feel the individual will perform the task.

Let the reference do most of the talking. Ask any follow-up questions if you feel the information is inadequate or does not complete the picture that you need to offer the individual the volunteer position.

QUICK OVERVIEW ON REFERENCE CHECKS

1. Reference checks need to be done on individuals who will be working with vulnerable customers (children, the elderly, or the handicapped) and in sensitive areas of the library (with computerized customer records or money).
2. The authority to request background and personal reference checks must come from your volunteer policy.
3. Determine the types of convictions that are unacceptable for purposes of hiring an individual in a particular position.
4. Prior research with your administration and attorney needs to be done on the legal ramifications of an individual with a criminal background who applies for a volunteer position.
5. All background checks must be done with the prior consent of the individual. Acquire or develop appropriate forms. Check with your local police department for procedural details.
6. Identify the administrative review process you will use when there are gray areas found in completed background reports or telephone reference checks.
7. Call personal or professional references to get more personalized, job-related information. A minimum of two references is usually adequate.
8. Information received from background checks and personal references must be kept strictly confidential and files must be maintained in a secure file cabinet.

SECTION
19

Volunteer Contracts and Releases

Volunteer contracts or agreements are used to add formality to the relationship between the volunteer and the library organization. The use of a contract shifts volunteering from a casual, "drop in when you can" approach to that of an expected commitment of scheduled time by the volunteer. The contract also stipulates that the library has committed resources to assist the volunteer in performing the assigned duties. Releases, on the other hand, are used when minors want to volunteer and need the approval of their parents or legal guardians. There are three basic parts to contracts and releases:

1. The library's responsibilities to the volunteer;
2. The volunteer's responsibilities to the library; and
3. The signature and date.

A sample volunteer agreement is found at sample 19-1.

THE LIBRARY'S RESPONSIBILITIES

Whether you title your library volunteer relationship a contract or an agreement, the first part of the document needs to specify the commitments your library is willing to make to volunteers. These commitments fall into the following five categories:

1. A safe work environment;
2. Appropriate information about the job;
3. Adequate training;

Welcome! The Douglas Public Library District is made up of five community branches, two satellites, and a Books-by-Mail Program. Your work as a volunteer provides important support for the library's mission of connecting the citizens of Douglas County with books and other informational resources.

Volunteer and paid staff of the Douglas Public Library District perform different work, are evaluated on different criteria, and receive different benefits.

The library agrees

1. To provide you, as a volunteer, with a safe work environment.
2. To provide supervision and training by a member of the library staff, who will answer your questions and provide feedback regarding your work.
3. To recognize your contributions as a volunteer to the success of the library.

As a volunteer, I agree

1. To accept the guidance and decisions of the staff.
2. To recognize the function of the paid staff, maintain smooth working relationships with them, and stay within the bounds of volunteer responsibilities.
3. To always wear a volunteer badge.
4. To report on time, as scheduled, and check in with the staff upon arrival at work. To record volunteer hours on the volunteer time sheet. To inform my supervisor as soon as possible if I am unable to keep my schedule. To notify my supervisor if I need to take an extended leave, if I wish to work in another location, or if I decide to resign.
5. To dress appropriately and act courteously to patrons and employees. (The library is a public place where attitude and appearance are important. Things need to be done accurately.)
6. To maintain the dignity and integrity of the library with the public and patron confidentiality, which is guaranteed under the Colorado Law. I will not discuss any patron by name or their reading selections outside of the library.

VOLUNTEER'S SIGNATURE	DATE	STAFF'S SIGNATURE	DATE

Please read, sign, and return with your volunteer application.

4. Sensitive and responsive supervision that includes feedback and evaluation on the work done; and

5. Recognition and respect for the volunteer.

In addition, you can include a sentence that states the volunteer is not receiving compensation for providing services to the library, and therefore is not an employee. This legal wording clarifies the role of the volunteer and protects the library. It makes it clear that the volunteer is not covered by any benefit plan, including workers' compensation, nor can she or he try to collect wages at some later date for service rendered to the library.

A safe work environment refers to all aspects of health and safety on the job. This includes appropriate supplies and equipment to accomplish the task, good lighting, adequate space, and so forth.

Each volunteer needs appropriate job information about the assigned tasks, a minimum amount of training, and basic information about the library procedures. Giving the volunteer this basic background information and training enables him or her to successfully accomplish the assigned work. If training is inadequate, the volunteer can be blamed for doing a poor job and she or he can, in turn, become unhappy with the work and quit. It is also essential for all volunteers to be told where to put their personal effects, where to take a break, or where to park their car.

Good supervision requires feedback, evaluation, and recognition. Managers who receive formal training or attend workshops learn these skills. However, it is the library staff member assigned to work with a volunteer that usually does not have this background. In some instances, even managers who have received formal managerial training may not practice what they have learned with staff or volunteers.

Recognition does not necessarily mean awards or certificates. It can take the form of calling volunteers by their names, giving them personalized greetings when they come to work, and making them feel a part of the library team.

VOLUNTEER RESPONSIBILITIES

The second part of the contract clarifies the commitments and responsibilities of the volunteer. The following are examples of these commitments:

1. Performs duties as assigned to the best of one's abilities;

2. Accepts guidance by the assigned staff member;

3. Adheres to the appropriate library rules and procedures by wearing a name badge, dressing appropriately, maintaining customer confidentiality, and acting courteously to customers and staff;

4. Reports at the scheduled time;

5. Gives prior notice to the staff supervisor if he or she expects to be absent or on extended leave;

6. Gives notice upon terminating; and

7. Identifies medical, health, or physical limitations related to the volunteer job.

The first three agreement phrases relate to job performance, supervision, and library rules. The volunteer commits to working under library standards and rules, including those relating to volunteers. How inclusive you want to be with the rules depends on your library director or legal counsel. On an informal basis, if a volunteer violates a rule, you can use the signed agreement to help you get cooperation. Failure to consistently follow the rules can be a basis for de-volunteering a person.

Items 4–6 relate to work schedules and reporting expected absences. Although volunteers are not paid for their time, they should adhere to time commitments and the procedures for handling absences. This compliance gives added importance to the volunteer-library relationship.

Medical, health, and physical limitations can be added as a separate part of the agreement. The issues here are twofold. First, there are the legal issues associated with volunteer injuries arising from not having taken the time to learn about a volunteer's health problem(s). Next, there is the human concern for the volunteer. You do not want to put a volunteer in an embarrassing or compromising situation because of your lack of knowledge about a health or medical problem.

SIGNATURE SECTION

The last part of the volunteer agreement is the signature and date lines. The representative of the library who signs the form may be you as the volunteer manager or the person who has delegated responsibility for the volunteer. Some forms of the agreement follow the wording of traditional legal documents with the phrase, "I acknowledge that I have read and fully understand the terms and conditions of the volunteer agreement."

The amount of formality in your agreement depends on your library administration. For any agreement, the key behind the signatures is the amount of mutual trust held by both parties. Volunteer agreements are used more like contracts signed in some schools between school officials and students concerning performance than like automobile purchase agreements. It is unlikely that you will take a volunteer to court based on the volunteer agreement. However, the agreement does clarify mutual expectations more than a mere information conversation.

WAIVERS AND RELEASES

A separate section in the volunteer agreement or a separate form may be constructed as a waiver from liability, depending on the legalistic qualities of your library. Essentially the volunteer agrees to "waive and hold harmless" the library from any liability occurring from an accident resulting in an injury to the volunteer or damage to personal property.

For example, you ask a volunteer to bring her laptop computer to the library to help you write invitations for a volunteer reception. As she walks across the library with her computer, she trips and falls down, breaking her laptop and twisting her knee. The estimated repair cost for the laptop is $650. Her doctor states that she may need a minor operation if a knee brace does not correct the problem.

In this example, there is no standard administrative practice that specifies what will happen. A signed waiver would on the surface seem to prevent the volunteer from suing the library for repair and medical costs. Some volunteers just admit they were clumsy and pay for the repair themselves (possibly from homeowner's insurance) and file a medical claim with their own heath insurance program. Others may want to sue the library to recover costs. Even with the signed waiver, because you asked the volunteer to bring the laptop to the library, the legal outcome is ambiguous.

Most volunteer release forms are used with young volunteers, those under the age of eighteen. These forms can carry the same information as the volunteer contracts, with an additional section for the parents or legal guardians to sign. The parents' signatures acknowledge that they know their child is volunteering at the library. Releases serve as legal protection for both the library and the parents. You are encouraged to use these forms (see samples 19-2, 19-3).

City of Aurora Library & Recreation Services
www.ci.aurora.co.us

Name _____   Birthday (month/day)_____

Address _____

City _____

State and Zip code _____

Telephone (H) _____

E-mail _____

Parents/guardian (include home and work numbers)   Mother _____

Father _____

Guardian _____

School _____   Grade _____   Age _____

Are you working towards community service hours? _____

Number of hours you would like to donate to the library: _____

Languages you speak fluently _____

Languages you read fluently _____

Skill/talents (please describe) _____

_____

Areas of interest _____

Availability

Days (please circle all that apply)   M   T   W   Th   F   S   Su

Times: Mornings _____

Afternoons _____

Are you available regularly every week? _____

Facility preference (circle choice):   Central   North   South

Have you had previous experience working in a library? If yes, please specify: _____

_____

I have read the job description and understand the responsibilities and duties of this position.

Signature of Applicant _____   Date:_____

Parents/ Guardian consent: _____(name of child) has my permission to participate in the library's volunteer program.

Signature of Parent/Guardian_____   Date:_____

Douglas
Public Library District

D   P   L   D

*(Parental permission is required of any
volunteer applicant who is under 14 years of age.)*

The Douglas Public Library District is more than happy to provide your child with a positive volunteer experience. The library staff are very busy people and while they do appreciate the help a young person can provide will take no responsibility for them should they decide to leave the job assignment or library facility.

It is our policy that a parent or legal guardian must remain in the library and work with volunteers under the age of twelve during their shift.

Volunteer's Name: _____

Phone: (303) _____   Date of birth: _____

Type of work to be performed: _____   _____

_____

Location: _____

Parent or Legal Guardian's Name: _____

Relationship to the applicant if other than parent:_____

_____

Parent or Guardian's signature _____   Date _____

SECTION
20

Time Forms

Time forms are used to keep track of volunteer hours. They are an important part of your record-keeping activity. As your volunteer pool grows, record keeping can also become a problem. Volunteers who need credit for working in the community (e.g., for school, social service organizations, or religious groups) tend to record their donated time faithfully. They have a good reason to keep track of their hours. Volunteers who freely give their time, however, do not always see the need for signing in or filling out one more form. They do not feel that recording their time is necessary if they are "donating" an hour or two.

REASONS FOR TIME FORMS

There are many reasons for tracking volunteer hours and keeping accurate records. We list some of the most important below:

To reward and recognize volunteers;

To credit supervising staff;

To evaluate your volunteer program;

To justify your program's value to the administration and staff;

To effectively publicize community involvement;

To support an individual's donated time for tax purposes, school credit, and so forth;

To document your volunteer program achievements; and

To document trends.

Your monthly or yearly reports are enhanced by the number of hours contributed by volunteers. Although volunteer hours only capture one aspect of a successful program, showing upward trends in the amount of time volunteers work lends additional credence to the value of your program. By multiplying the hours contributed by an estimated dollar value of volunteer time, you can demonstrate a bottom-line indicator of the impact the program has on the library. This dollar figure can be a double-edged sword. If too much emphasis is placed on the value of volunteer dollars, administrators can use these figures during tight budget periods to replace paid staff or not hire additional staff. These decisions can encourage negative perceptions of volunteers by the staff that in turn can make your job harder.

Calculating year-to-date and lifetime volunteer hours is one popular way of recognizing volunteers. Which hours to count can be somewhat ambiguous. For example, how would you track a volunteer's hours if she works on a project at home or if she bakes a cake for a staff and volunteer recognition event? In either case, the volunteer may not think about completing a form for hours worked at home. The library may actually "lose" hours relative to the volunteer who is working in the library. One option is to have volunteers include their work at home if it exceeds four hours a month.

Staff working with volunteers can be given special recognition. Even if supervising volunteers is part of their job description, you can still send them a thank-you letter or present them with a small gift. It's also important to include this information in their yearly performance evaluation or write a letter for their personnel file.

Time forms are important for documenting the hours of court-directed volunteers or volunteers working for school or institutional credit. Also, there are community programs that need documented time for an individual to purchase food at a discount or receive tax relief. In each case, the time form acts like a legal document by providing proof that the volunteer worked the assigned hours. To maintain accuracy, it is important to have the volunteer and supervisor sign the form to verify that the hours were completed as assigned. In large libraries, security issues may also be a concern. Accurate time forms can tell who was in the building at a certain time and where they were working.

Finally, tracking volunteer hours gives you the opportunity to find out who is not coming in as scheduled. This is important if you have multiple departments or multiple locations and the volunteer or library staff does not call you with the information. By reviewing time forms, you can see a pattern of absences. You can use this information to find out why a volunteer is not coming in.

TYPES OF TIME FORMS

There are three types of time forms. The first is the daily or weekly sign-in roster where the volunteers sign in and out on the dates they worked. One variation is to have the task(s) they worked on listed as well as the name of the assigned staff supervisor. From the volunteer's perspective, this is an easy process as long as the sign-in sheets are readily available. From the manager's perspective, it takes only a glance to know which volunteers are working. The negative aspect of this form is that it can result in a loss of confidentiality because anyone can review the names and the hours. Furthermore, it is more difficult to sort out

the total number of hours by volunteer if you use a sheet that includes a week at a time, especially if you have many volunteers working on different days (see samples 20-1 and 20-2).

The second type of time form is the monthly calendar (see sample 20-3). This form has the volunteer's name written next to the date and time that he or she is expected to work. A check mark next to the name indicates that the volunteer reported for work. This system works if volunteers are on a regular schedule with a set time each month.

The third approach is separate time sheets or cards for each volunteer. The volunteer is expected to complete the time card and put it back in the file box on the dates worked. If a volunteer does not want to keep track of his or her hours, you may have to fill in a card to complete your reporting requirements.

PROCEDURES

It is important that you specify whether the time forms are to be completed on a daily, weekly, or monthly basis. Will one manager be responsible for sending you the time forms, or will each staff member who supervises a volunteer send them to you? Will you collect them yourself? Additionally, who will make sure that forms for the next time period are put out for volunteers and who will to let you know if there is a shortage of forms? Finally, who will keep and update the statistical information?

SAMPLE 20-1
Volunteer Sign-in Sheet

(Please print)   Originating Branch/Department: _____

Date	Time In	Name of Volunteer	Activity/Assignment	Time Out	Total Time

Please return to DPL Volunteer Office at the end of each month.

Dougles
Public Library District

D   P   L   D

High School Graduation Required
Community Service Schedule Agreement

_____: Your community service hours with the Douglas

Public Library District have been scheduled at the _____ Branch.
You have been scheduled as follows:

Sunday: _____

Monday: _____

Tuesday: _____

Wednesday: _____

Thursday: _____

Friday: _____

Saturday: _____

Sunday: _____

> If you are not able to work your scheduled time, contact:
>
> _____ at:
>
> _____.
> If they are not available, please leave a message.

Note: Failure to show up for an assigned work shift without calling, can and will lead to termination of services, as we have people waiting to get into the program.

STAFF NOTE: Please make a copy of this agreement and file it in the
5″ × 8″ volunteer file box.

Dougles
Public Library District

D   P   L   D

High School Graduation Required
Community Service Schedule Agreement

_____: Your community service hours with the Douglas

Public Library District have been scheduled at the _____ Branch.
You have been scheduled as follows:

Sunday: _____

Monday: _____

Tuesday: _____

Wednesday: _____

Thursday: _____

Friday: _____

Saturday: _____

Sunday: _____

> If you are not able to work your scheduled time, contact:
>
> _____ at:
>
> _____.
> If they are not available, please leave a message.

Note: Failure to show up for an assigned work shift without calling, can and will lead to termination of services, as we have people waiting to get into the program.

STAFF NOTE: Please make a copy of this agreement and file it in the
5″ × 8″ volunteer file box.

SAMPLE 20-3
Douglas Public Library District
Volunteer Hours

January 2002

Please report to the nearest 1/4 hour

Name	1	2	3	4	5	6	7	8	9	10	11	12	13	14	15	16	17	18	19	20	21	22	23	24	25	26	27	28	29	30	31	Total

Civic/Social
School
Friends
Community

SECTION

21

Orientation Training

Many people find new work experiences disorienting and confusing. This holds true for new volunteers, especially when they are placed in jobs with few or no introductions to staff or other volunteers, no discussion of library policies, or no instructions about where to put their personal belongings. Orientation training bridges the gap from a volunteer being an "outsider" to a "member of the team." When orientation is done properly, the new volunteer will develop camaraderie with staff and other volunteers.

Orientation training can be either informal or formal and as limited or detailed in content as you feel necessary to adequately acquaint the individual with the job and the library. If you work for a small library, the first day can be as simple as making introductions to staff and other volunteers, providing a brief tour of the library, including the location of the rest room, and explaining where to put personal items. In a large library with many volunteers and job opportunities, orientation can be done in a group setting on a monthly or quarterly basis.

As you think through the process of orientating a volunteer to your library system, consider the following points:

Orientation format;

Orientation session;

Orientation packet and checklist; and

Three-month follow-up.

ORIENTATION FORMAT

Orientation training should not be confused with skill or job training. Orientation gives volunteers their first general introduction to the behind-the-scenes operations of the library. It also enables volunteers to meet the staff. As you plan the format for the orientation session, you need to decide on the length of the session and the time and day during the week. These decisions often depend on the number of new volunteers and whether or not they have paying jobs. If you have a large number of new volunteers, you can hold a monthly orientation for about two to three hours. You might want to include additional time for refreshments and a tour of the library. If you have a large number of young volunteers, you can hold an after-school orientation with fewer handouts and more food. When there are a few new volunteers, you can conduct personal orientations at the time they join. The orientation can be up to one hour in length, including time for questions and answers.

As you put together your final format for either a large group or individual sessions, it is important to decide which library handouts, brochures, manuals, task lists, and other information the volunteers need to have to be well informed. Recognize that too much information can create information overload and much of what you say will not be remembered a week later. The materials should be viewed as reference items that can be referred to later on. As you prepare the handouts, ask a staff member for his or her input on the professionalism of the material. Poorly copied or hard-to-read materials do not make a good first impression. If you are going to use flip charts or slides during your group presentations, be sure the information is current and accurate.

Finally, think through the session by writing notes for yourself, mentally orchestrating the session so that you can "see" it flow from topic to topic. It is important that individuals leave with the feeling they have made a good decision in becoming library volunteers.

ORIENTATION SESSION

Regardless of how informal or formal your orientation is, you need to cover the following points: general welcome, staff/volunteer introductions, library expectations, name badges, library tour, and relevant policies (this can be handled by an orientation packet).

General Welcome

The welcome should reflect genuine sincerity and friendliness. This is important because it leaves a lasting impression and makes the new volunteer feel immediately appreciated and part of the library team. A "welcoming letter" (see sample 21-1) is a good beginning.

During a group session, keep the opening comments brief and to the point. Give a general overview of the orientation to keep yourself and the group on track. Time is valuable to you and the new volunteers. In addition, they are probably eager to get started with their new jobs.

Introductions

New volunteers need to be introduced to the supervising staff, staff members who work with the volunteers, and other volunteers. You can have several of these people available at the meeting or introduce them later during the tour. The supervising staff should include the immediate supervisor and the facility manager. Introducing these people gives the volunteer a sense of the library's organizational structure and how they fit into the larger picture and operations of the library.

If the volunteer is working with other staff members, it is important to introduce him or her to them so that she or he is acknowledged as part

Welcome to the Douglas Public Library District!

Thank you for your willingness to volunteer your time, talents, and energies to help make our library the best it can be.

The vision for public library services in Douglas County began in 1966 when the county commissioners responded to public requests by establishing a library fund of $5,000. At the first Library Board meeting, Philip S. Miller and his wife donated $25,000 for library building construction. Services began in 1967 consisting of a rented building in Castle Rock, the basement of the Methodist Church in Parker and a countywide bookmobile service. In 1968 a new library was built in Castle Rock at 303 Gilbert Street. That building was known as the "Douglas County Public Library." There were 842 regular patrons. By 1971, talk began of the need to expand the library in Castle Rock. In 1987 the Philip S. Miller Library was opened at its present location. In 1984 the Oakes Mill Library was opened in Lone Tree, donated by a land developer. That building has since been demolished, rebuilt, and reopened in October 1998 under the name of Lone Tree Public Library. Meanwhile the Parker Library moved to a building on Main Street in 1985 and on to its present location in 1995. Louviers had a volunteer-run library for many years. It later became a part of the Douglas County Library System. The Highlands Ranch Library originally was a joint effort with the Northridge Elementary School. In 1991 it moved to its present location. A new library building is being planned in the Highlands Ranch Town Center with opening planned for the year 2000. The original Douglas County Public Library System officially became the Douglas Public Library District (DPLD) in 1990 as a result of a countywide vote. At that time, voters approved the formation of an independent library district funded by a 2.75 mill levy.

DPLD is currently made up of five community libraries, two school satellite locations, a homebound delivery program and a Books-by-Mail program. DPLD currently has over 72,000 patrons. As a volunteer, you contribute significantly to the community through a wide variety of interesting and fulfilling activities.

Your work as a volunteer provides important support for the library mission of encouraging everyone in the community to establish a lifelong habit of reading. We strive to provide the citizens of Douglas County with public access to books, tapes, and other informational resources.

We hope your time with us will be mutually satisfying to both the library and yourself. Should you have any needs or concerns about your role with us feel free to contact:

Willo Auger
Volunteer Services Coordinator
961 Plum Creek Blvd.
Castle Rock, CO 80104
303-688-8752

of the group. Finally, if there are other volunteers working in the same area or at the same time, it is a good idea to make connections with others who can relate to the new volunteer; this makes the adjustment period more comfortable and completes the picture of a "volunteer-friendly" library.

Name Badges

A name badge gives the volunteer an immediate sense of identification with the library staff as well as identifying her as a volunteer. A badge allows the new volunteer to move about freely, especially in staff-only areas. An important side benefit to using special volunteer badges is the positive publicity that is generated by an individual wearing one in a public area.

Facility Tour

Provide a tour of the library that includes both the public and staff work areas. This gives the volunteer a picture of the library and helps the individual transition from an outsider to an effective volunteer.

ORIENTATION PACKET AND CHECKLIST

An orientation packet can include library brochures, information on library services, and a handbook. A volunteer handbook is a good way to demonstrate professionalism in your program. The handbook can be used as an orientation outline when you go over the various sections with new volunteers. In addition, an orientation check sheet is useful in helping you make sure you cover all the pertinent points.

A handbook can be as simple as a few pages stapled or bound together in a colorful spiral-bound booklet. The handbook contains both general information items and specific procedures that affect the volunteer work experience. Under "general information" you can include:

Library history;

Volunteer mission statement;

Library services and events;

Confidentiality policy;

Rights of a library volunteer;

Organizational chart;

Key contacts;

Key telephone numbers;

Glossary of library terms (jargon);

Emergency procedures; and

Map of library (including location of rest rooms and break rooms).

Some of the general information can come directly from staff handbooks, library brochures and handouts, training manuals, and the library policy and procedure manual (appropriate sections in this book will also give you ideas about what to include in the volunteer handbook).

Procedural information that is useful for new volunteers to know includes:

Volunteer schedule;

Volunteer assignments;

Sample time forms;

Absence and late notification procedures;

Name badge policy;

Storage of personal items;

Parking;

Use of the telephone for personal calls;

Breaks;

Performance appraisal;

Volunteer benefits; and

Volunteer awards.

In this section, you can parallel the staff handbook and find additional ideas from relevant sections. A volunteer will not remember all of this information, so design the handbook as a training/reference guide that can be referred to for useful information when necessary.

If you do not choose to use a handbook, you can develop a packet of information in a loose-leaf folder. This folder can include sheets of pertinent information such as the job description, a map of the library, and a one-page sheet on general volunteer policies.

THREE-MONTH FOLLOW-UP

It is important to follow the initial orientation with a three-month phone call or meeting to find out how the volunteer is doing and his or her level of job satisfaction. In addition, you can get an evaluation from the supervisor. This will give you a clearer picture about how the volunteer is performing.

A three-month time period gives the volunteer adequate time to fit into the library organization. If it is not working out, you can head off future problems that could reflect poorly on the volunteer or the program. This time period also allows you to decide if retraining would be useful or if an assignment to another library job would be more appropriate. In an extreme case, if the volunteer is not working out, you may have to de-volunteer him or her.

SECTION
22

Customer Confidentiality

New library volunteers rarely get to see a copy of the American Library Association's *Library Bill of Rights* or "Statement of Professional Ethics," or learn about the library's obligation to ensure that the records of a customer are kept confidential. Many do not understand that there is a privacy issue in sharing information with a friend about someone's request for a certain book or discussing what a particular customer is checking out. Most have no concept of confidentiality issues. Therefore, the following key areas should be taken into account when designing your volunteer program:

Policy on confidentiality;

Training for specific jobs; and

Restricted volunteer jobs.

POLICY ON CONFIDENTIALITY

Your library probably has a written policy on customer confidentiality (also known as patron privacy) as part of the staff employment handbook or library policy and procedural manual. If this is the case, you need to include it in your volunteer orientation handbook or make it a separate handout for new volunteers. The policy can be discussed on an informal basis or as part of a formal orientation program. A state law on confidentiality and privacy may also govern the library. You can refer to this law to reinforce the importance of the library policy.

As the volunteer manager, your job is to make sure the volunteers understand the importance of this policy and the consequences of not following it, including de-volunteering.

TRAINING FOR SPECIFIC JOBS

Volunteers who work in public service areas with homebound delivery of books, books-by-mail programs, or at the circulation or readers' advisory desks will have access to customer records. They need to understand that the information made available to them carries an obligation to maintain confidentiality, be discreet, and use professional objectivity.

RESTRICTED VOLUNTEER JOBS

Your library may restrict volunteers, by policy or by practice, from positions that require working with customer records. This kind of restriction reduces the chance that a volunteer may unwittingly share information about a customer. If this is the case in your library, it is still important for all volunteers to understand the basis for customer confidentiality and abide by the policy.

Every library volunteer is subject to the customer privacy policies of the library, whether or not they are assigned duties that include access to a customer's personal information, borrowing records, or material requests. Further, every volunteer is prohibited from using information about staff or volunteers for personal gain or to benefit members of other organizations. Violation of this policy is grounds for de-volunteering.

Note: If your state has a customer privacy/confidentiality law with stated financial penalties for violation, this information can be added to the above policy statement.

ALTERNATIVE POLICY

As a volunteer you may gain access to privileged information about library customers. You may not share this information with anyone except library staff, including family members, friends, and neighbors. You may not use any listing of staff or volunteers for personal gain or to benefit an organization. Violation of this policy is automatically grounds for de-volunteering.

SECTION
23

Volunteer Skill Training

The basic component of every assigned task is the element of job skill training. Even the most mundane task can be done incorrectly without proper training. For this reason, when planning a volunteer training component, the following key issues need to be addressed:

Trainer identification;

Definition of the scope and limits of the job;

On-the-job training; and

Specialized training.

TRAINER IDENTIFICATION

Who should train the volunteers is a question that depends on the knowledge, time, and mentoring abilities of available staff. As a volunteer manager, you may have had prior experience, or you may have general library knowledge about how to perform particular tasks. You probably can teach some volunteer jobs, such as shelving, shelf reading, magazine sorting, and other similar tasks. If you are busy, you may have to delegate this work to a supervising staff member. He or she may not have the time or patience to properly show the volunteer how to get the job done. Without the feeling of comfort that comes from understanding job expectations, the volunteer experience can easily get off to a poor start.

In addition, there are semispecialized skills, such as inspecting audiovisual material for damage, filing serial updates, or working a book sale, that need specialized knowledge that you may not have to properly train the volunteer. In these situations, you need a staff member who works in the specific area. Here too the selection of a person to train and mentor the volunteer is critical to the success of your program. There are staff members who become curt when an individual does not immediately understand what to do after a quick explanation, or does not explain details about how to handle the exceptions. Some staff members may even feel it is not their job to train others, including volunteers. It is important to identify people who are willing and able to be good trainers for your volunteers.

DEFINING THE SCOPE AND LIMITS OF THE JOB

The scope of the work needs to be identified by a job description or a task card so that the volunteer understands the defined limits. For example, a volunteer is assigned the job of answering all directional questions at an information desk. The specific duties are first defined in a written job description. Then the department manager trains the volunteer to distinguish between directional, reference, and ready-reference questions at the desk and how to refer a customer to the appropriate area or a specific staff member. The volunteer should be well equipped to answer questions and stay within the scope of the assigned task. If she or he chooses to ignore the job limits, the result is poor customer service because she or he has no specialized training.

Volunteers, like paid staff, need to understand why there are limits to their work. If they have difficulty grasping this concept or working within their present boundaries, you can train them in another job or de-volunteer them.

ON-THE-JOB TRAINING

Most of your volunteers will learn on the job. Adults will learn better if they have a chance to practice their new skills after the initial training period. The volunteer who is shown the procedures to follow in selecting and processing uncataloged paperbacks, or how to run a complex photocopier, will retain information and be more successful if there is a supervised practice period. Moreover, it is important for the equipment, tools, and work space to be available from the beginning. It is very difficult for a volunteer to be successful if there is no room to work or a piece of equipment is unavailable or broken.

Volunteers coming in with specialized skills, such as knowledge of specific databases or desktop publishing packages, will still need to be trained in library terminology and project expectations. In this case, the training is not about specific skills but about project goals.

SPECIALIZED TRAINING

Some volunteer positions will require more specialized training. Mending books, literacy tutoring, or processing archival material will require training by a staff person in that department. In this situation, it is useful to review the volunteer's work early in the process to make sure the job is being done correctly and any problem areas are properly and quickly corrected.

In any specialized job, it is very important to make sure your selection process identifies volunteers who are not only willing to work, but have the skills and aptitude to perform at the standards set by the library. If the volunteer does not work at an acceptable level, it is better to offer him or her another opportunity than to hope for long-term improvement.

If the job requires public contact, such as "greeters" at an information desk or assistants at children's programs, then it is important to include some training on what volunteers can say and how to say it. By preparing scripts and practicing different scenarios, you can make sure there is some consistency in training. If you write the script, it is a good idea to have the appropriate department manager review it first. Remember that scripting cannot cover all the situations a volunteer will experience, but it can help an individual understand what needs to be said in many customer interactions. Do not forget to include in your training session what cannot be said to the public. For example, "I understand that you're upset that the library does not have your book. They don't seem to want to order the kind of books that I think you and I like to read." The volunteer in this instance may have good intentions, but the phrasing certainly does not help the image of the library. Good scripting and practice can usually prevent this kind of unfortunate exchange from happening.

When volunteers enjoy working with your customers, they will usually be able to learn the script quickly and adapt to changing circumstances.

TYPE OF TRAINING

Orientation Check Sheet

A check sheet enables the coordinator to make sure a new volunteer has the necessary information and equipment to begin the job. This list may include the following: a volunteer badge, location of rest rooms and storage areas for personal belongings, the name and phone number of her supervisor, introduction to staff and other volunteers, etc.

Written Scripts

Scripts are useful when a volunteer is assigned to a task that needs uniform and consistent statements, particularly when working with the public, for example, greeting customers at the library entrance or answering telephones. A script can be as simple as, "Home Town Public Library, how may I direct your call?"

Task Completion Checklist

This is a list of subtasks that need to be completed as part of an assigned job that stretches over many days. The list has a place for the volunteer to "x" or initial so that progress toward completing the whole job can be monitored and the volunteer knows where to begin the tasks on each workday.

Short Demonstrations with Practice Session

"Showing by doing" is one of the best forms of training because it gives a volunteer a chance to practice a new skill. For example, donated books can be divided into categories such as textbooks and general nonfiction books. You can demonstrate to the volunteer which category each book belongs in and then let the volunteer practice the sorting technique. This exemplifies applied learning.

Cheat Sheets

These task aids are written in an abbreviated format to help one's memory in the performance of occasional tasks. For the volunteer who enters data on a monthly computer report, particular commands can be listed on a sheet so that she or he can remember the nuances of inputting the information.

Visual Display of a Job

These are pictures of how a set of tasks should be accomplished. For a volunteer assigned to set up a community meeting room, labeled pictures of the various room arrangements can be posted so that a group can ask for configuration 1, 2, or 3, etc. This reduces the chances for error. A new volunteer can be asked to set up a room based upon the pictured configurations.

Graphics Aids

These are often illustrations from computer graphics software that are used to help explain a set of tasks. To illustrate, a volunteer who is teaching library customers Internet search techniques, can have a prepared set of graphics to use as a way to be sure to cover all the points.

Videotapes

The "how to" videotapes are training aids that can be reviewed to help one learn skilled techniques. For example, a video on how to mend books could be watched by a volunteer who is going to do general mending. Usually these kinds of videos include a written instructional aid that can be used separately.

Flip Charts

A simple flip chart is useful to list or diagram key points of a task or locations in a building. If a volunteer is assigned to help shift shelves, the flip chart can show where the call numbers will be relocated.

Tutorials

Software programs often come with tutorials. Volunteers can be asked to use the tutorial to learn a software program that they will be working on as part of an assigned duty.

Reminder Signs

These are briefly worded signs to serve as memory aids, such as, "wash hands after using cleaning solvents," or "return office equipment to supply room" or "did you sign in?" These signs, sealed in plastic, can be posted or given to a volunteer on a job assignment.

Two-Minute Training Sessions

Quick training requires the spoken words to be supplemented with one or more training aids, such as a demonstration or short practice session and a follow-up. This allows the introduction of a task, the practice of performing the task, and some tool for remembering the order of activities to complete the task. For example, asking a volunteer to make two-sided copies and collating the pages into a booklet on a large commercial copier is best accomplished with a demonstration, short practice session, and a cheat sheet on what to do when the copier jams.

SECTION

24

Safety Training

Safety training needs to be a part of your volunteer orientation and part of the ongoing practice of updating information. Training does not necessarily mean formal classroom instruction but includes informal conversations on correct safety procedures. When you take a minute to show a volunteer the correct way to use a paper cutter, this is safety training. When a volunteer gets a finger too close to the cutter and slices some skin off, this is an accident, and often a failure in safety training.

The first step in safety training is to look over your volunteer tasks and determine what kinds of training information should be shared with the volunteers. Then review the library's safety manual (if there is one) to see if there are sections that concern volunteers. Copy this information for your volunteer handbook or use it as a separate handout. As you go through this information, there are five key areas to be aware of:

1. Library safety policies and procedures;
2. Accident notification and reports;
3. Protective equipment;
4. Specialized safety training; and
5. Health and wellness information.

LIBRARY SAFETY POLICIES AND PROCEDURES

Your library probably has a formal safety policy statement. This statement can set the tone for your conversations with volunteers. Safety practices are inherent in every job and an awareness of safety issues is extremely important in preventing accidents. You may have an accident-prone volunteer, but in most instances an accident is a momentary lapse in doing a job correctly. For example, a capable volunteer carelessly puts the book cleaner down and the solvent splashes in her face and eyes. Although she knows she was not paying attention, you or the supervisor have to deal with an accident.

If the library has safety procedures for each department, you may find it useful to review these and provide handouts with your comments to volunteers working in those departments. What would be most useful to you is to take a few minutes to go over the safety aspects of each volunteer's job. This may be as simple as showing a volunteer how to properly adjust a chair, including the back support, at a computer terminal. If you do not feel comfortable training a volunteer in safety techniques, ask the immediate supervisor to work with him or her. In this way, the volunteer knows that the library takes safety procedures seriously.

ACCIDENT NOTIFICATION AND REPORTS

When an accident happens, volunteers follow different procedures than paid staff, who are covered by workers' compensation. Staff members are told which clinic to visit and which forms to fill out. A volunteer would go to her own clinic or doctor. On the other hand, if your volunteer was incapacitated and you did not have a contact name or the name of her doctor or clinic, your best option would be to call 911.

Even if you were not required to complete any forms for a volunteer accident, it is important to have an in-house "Incident Report" that could be completed by you and the supervising staff member indicating what happened. In the event there is later legal action, you have documented the time of the accident, the sequence of events, the actions taken, and the names of any witnesses.

If you do have an emergency contact name and phone number (this should be included on your application for volunteer service), you need to keep it in a convenient place and decide who can access this information. You may want to leave a copy of current volunteer contacts at a library manager's desk and make it available to the person in charge.

PROTECTIVE EQUIPMENT

Most library tasks do not require protective safety equipment or clothing. If volunteers are using glue and solvents, you can have disposable gloves available to protect their hands. You can also provide wrist support pads to place under computer keyboards, work gloves for pulling weeds, or a sturdy ladder for hanging a picture.

After a disaster, such as a flood, protective aprons, boots, gloves, and disposable respiratory masks should be made available to anyone involved in the cleanup process. Also, if a volunteer sorts through a donation of books, you need to provide gloves and disposable masks to address the possibility of dust and insect excrement.

Finally, if you have a safety officer in the library or have access to a risk control specialist from your workers' compensation insurance carrier, you can get free advice on workplace safety as it relates to any volunteer tasks.

SPECIALIZED SAFETY TRAINING

Specialized safety training is the exception in libraries. Cardiopulmonary resuscitation (CPR), first aid, and learning to use a fire extinguisher come closest to what is considered "specialized training." If this type of training is available to the staff, it might be important to also include long-term volunteers. However, talk to your safety officer or key administrator first and find out how medical emergencies are handled in your library. It is essential to know if a trained library volunteer or a volunteer trained as a registered nurse can expose the library to a legal risk if he or she provides emergency first aid. If so, is this risk acceptable to the library administration?

HEALTH AND WELLNESS INFORMATION

If your library has a wellness manual for staff, it would be useful to share this information with your volunteers. Some manuals not only show the proper way to lift boxes, but also illustrate a quick on-the-job exercise to reduce fatigue and body stress. Even though your volunteers may work only a few hours a week, sharing this kind of information shows you care about their well-being and want to help them prevent personal injuries.

Breaks

Taking breaks can actually help increase productivity. When you feel stressed out, fatigued, or like you are moving in slow motion after doing the same task for a long period of time, take a short break.

MICROBREAKS

Use microbreaks to give your eyes and muscles a change of pace. If you have been looking at a computer screen for an extended period, focus your eyes on some distant object for five seconds. Take a few deep breaths and shift position.

MINIBREAKS

Short, five-minute minibreaks can include stretching or changing job tasks to use different sets of muscles. If you have been unloading book carts, answering telephones, or performing any other tasks for an extended period of time, take a minibreak.

RELAXATION BREAKS

Use any assigned, scheduled breaks to reduce stress in the following ways:

Slowly and deeply inhale through the nose and then slowly exhale through the mouth.

Read a joke book.

Progressively tense different muscle groups for five seconds and let your body go limp for thirty seconds.

Visualize a peaceful scene, a fun event, or a pleasant activity.

Handling Books and Materials

Handling library materials can involve lifting, bending, pushing, carrying, and reaching activities. In particular, lifting library materials from a book drop, books from shelves, or moving tables to set up for meetings can involve your back, legs, shoulders, and arms. Good lifting techniques require the following: (1) plan before you lift; (2) keep your back in a natural, upright position; (3) bend and lift with your legs, keeping the items lifted close to your body; and (4) if you must turn, pivot your feet without twisting at the waist. If an object is heavy or looks heavy, get assistance.

Safe Work Habits

As a library volunteer, remember to practice basic safety techniques when performing library tasks. These include the following:

Use step stools for books and objects in high places.

Use only the top two shelves of a book truck to avoid back and arm strain.

When moving and shifting books, use both hands and do not overextend your grip and reach.

Do not stack books and miscellaneous items on the floor or on top of computers.

Keep often-used equipment within easy reach. Remove clutter from your work space.

When sitting, turn the chair rather than twisting your body.

Do not rest your wrists and forearms on sharp edges.

When using the telephone, be careful not to bend your neck.

Computer Workstations

When you are working at the computer for a long period of time, your neck, back, shoulders, legs, hands, wrist, fingers, and eyes are the areas of the body where most of the activity (or inactivity) occurs. Remember to take short breaks to reduce stress to these body parts. If your computer is used by others, learn how to make the necessary adjustments in chair height and tilt of the screen to prevent glare. Request help from a staff person to make the necessary adjustments.

Reducing Life's Stressors

Minimizing your stressors is a skill that can be learned and practiced. The sources of most stressors are threefold: (1) burnout from too much activity, (2) interpersonal relationships and conflicts, and (3) personal worries, feelings of inadequacy, or being too demanding on oneself or others. The following are various ways to reduce stress.

- Quiet Time

    Plan a quiet period in your day without noise or interruption.

    Stay a few minutes in your car without the radio or cell phone on.

- Do something different in your daily routine.

    Take a different way home or take a walk in a new area of town.

    Visit a friend you have not seen for a while.

- Do something that is fun for you.

    Try a new hobby or participate in a sport or recreational activity.

    Read books or magazines you have not seen or read before.

- Get outside help.

    Seek help from a counselor, the clergy, or other professional.

    Hire someone to do jobs that are causing you extreme stress.

- Personal Practices and Outlooks

    Establish realistic daily schedules, accepting the fact that unexpected events will occur.

    Realize that for most activities, adequacy, not perfection, is the goal.

    Practice positive self-talk: "I can do this." "I look good."

    Find the humor in situations and remember to smile.

SECTION
25

Performance Evaluation

An evaluation interview is a focused, two-way conversation designed to elicit and share information after a designated period of time on the job. The issue of whether or not to evaluate library volunteers and who should do it can be a very touchy subject. Most volunteers want to do a good job. If they are told their work will be subject to a written evaluation, they may reconsider volunteer work. On the other hand, written evaluations can be useful in helping an individual improve or enabling you to find a better job fit for the volunteer.

If volunteers are going to be given performance evaluations, they should be given this information at the beginning of the interview process. This can be positively phrased in the following manner: "All employees, including volunteers, must go through an evaluation process. This is done to show areas of individual strength and indicate areas that need improvement to optimize your performance." If a potential volunteer does not choose to work within this type of structured environment, it is important to find out as early as possible.

Before deciding to implement performance evaluations, consider the following:

Purpose of evaluations;

Process of evaluations;

Complexity of the forms;

Library staff or outside evaluators; and

Frequency of evaluations.

PURPOSE OF EVALUATIONS

Evaluations are an important part of any job. They are one way to measure the growth and productivity of an individual as well as to make him or her account-

105

able for time and effort. In terms of a volunteer, evaluations can be used to:

Provide feedback about task performances;

Learn about a volunteer's experience as well as his or her feelings about the program;

Develop positive comments about a volunteer for use in recognition programs;

Explore new jobs in the library that may be more suitable to an individual's skills or interests;

Suggest other organizations that might provide a better volunteer fit; and

Provide feedback to the originating agency for volunteers performing court restitution or service learning.

THE PROCESS OF EVALUATIONS

Formal Evaluations

Formal evaluations are done after a volunteer has spent two to three months on the job. A general form can be provided to the supervisor for writing brief comments about the volunteer's job performance. A second form can be given to the volunteer to determine if the initial training is adequate, if there are enough supplies to get the job done, if the assigned day and time are working out, and whether she or he is receiving the necessary help from supervisors and staff. After reviewing the evaluations, you can call a meeting to go over the results. At this time you can include an open-ended discussion on any concerns or questions the volunteer may have, and then at a later date follow up with a written note or a second meeting to clarify any unanswered questions raised during the meeting.

If you receive any negative comments from department supervisors or staff, your job will be to share this information with the volunteer in a positive and constructive manner. It is not uncommon in this situation to ignore or talk around problems in performance. If you need to discuss a problem, do it factually. Concentrate on job performance and job behavior. It might help to script the conversation first so that you can carefully think about what you are going to say and how you will say it. Be as positive as you can.

Informal Evaluations

If you do not use formal evaluation forms, let the volunteer know that the purpose of this meeting is to share information about his or her overall volunteer experience. Indicate that this is a routine conversation with all volunteers after two or three months of working at the library. Your goal is to seek ways to improve the volunteer experience and to make sure that your recruitment interviewing statements about the volunteer tasks still hold true. In this way, both of you learn from the conversation.

A semiformal evaluation can be conducted by calling the supervising staff person and asking key questions about the volunteer's work performance. Your written notes become the basis for the evaluation comments. It is important to frame your questions to the staff person in a neutral manner so that you are not biasing the responses. Ask questions such as, "Can you tell me how Molly is working out cleaning books? Give me some examples of her routine when she comes in to work." If the staff member merely says "she's doing okay," then use a probing question to find out more specific details. For example, "Does she make sure she has enough supplies for the day? If not, what does she do?" These questions can lead to specific examples of Molly's performance.

COMPLEXITY OF FORMS

Written evaluation forms can be as simple as four or five questions with spaces for comments or they can contain statements that allow a staff member to check off answers under evaluation categories. The second form is easy to use and gives you general information about a volunteer. However, this type of evaluation can lead to ambiguous interpretation of the answers. You cannot be sure what one staff member means by the word *seldom* or *always*. There are too many variables in the workplace to make a simple "check-the-box" evaluation form effective. More sophisticated forms that list a wide range of specific performance behaviors, and provide space for a written assessment of these behaviors, are more useful. These forms usually yield better information about how well the volunteer is doing.

LIBRARY STAFF AND OUTSIDE EVALUATORS

Who should evaluate a volunteer? It can be you if you are overseeing the volunteer or it can be the supervising staff member who has regular contact with the volunteer. However, if the volunteer is working under a library supervisor but performs his or her job off-site, such as taking books to senior centers or reading to children at a local day-care center, you may need input from a second-party evaluator. An off-site supervisor can be used in two ways: (1) to evaluate the individual volunteer, or (2) to evaluate the program that includes a component for volunteer evaluations. Either approach is useful but both have problems.

In the first approach, a "problem" volunteer will likely be brought to your attention; this is not a foregone conclusion, however, even if you ask for honest evaluations. Sometimes second-party supervisors are hesitant to criticize volunteers because they represent the library and feel they may lose the services you provide. It is very important to have good rapport with an agency representative. In other cases, the agency representative may be the problem and not your volunteer.

Your knowledge of the relationship is very important in interpreting the evaluation.

A second problem with an evaluation that focuses on the individual volunteer is that you may not be getting information about the program as a whole. The volunteers may be doing a great job, but the outreach program may have outlived its usefulness or need revamping.

The second evaluation approach is to focus on the program's strengths and weaknesses, with a secondary emphasis on the volunteers. This information is useful for planning recruitment strategies and program development, but may not give you adequate feedback about the abilities of individual volunteers.

If you do choose to accept a second-party evaluation, you need to decide how much weight you want to place on library staff evaluations versus the comments of the outside evaluator. Probably only a small number of volunteers will be involved in off-site work; nevertheless you need to know how they are doing.

FREQUENCY OF EVALUATIONS

After conducting an initial evaluation after one month (see sample 25-1), you should plan on some form of annual evaluation. You might want to review your records to determine how long most volunteers stay with the library. If the majority leave after eight to nine months, probably you want to perform only one performance review. If you have a core group of individuals that have been working for several years, you would want to perform a yearly evaluation. This is quality time with the volunteer. Even if your comments are positive, this focused conversation can be a good way for volunteers to share ideas with you about the program or their evolving interests. Just taking the time to conduct an evaluation demonstrates that you and the library respect the volunteer's skills, talents, and energies that are freely given.

ONE-MONTH VOLUNTEER EVALUATION FORM

Name_____ Work Location _____

Assignment _____ Supervisor _____

Beginning Date _____ Date of Orientation _____

Daytime Phone _____ Best time to call _____

☐ Relationship to supervisor:

☐ Relationship to team members:

☐ Response to work load (too much or too little):

☐ Response to hours:

☐ Quality of on-the-job training:

☐ Job strengths:

☐ Job weakness or areas of improvement:

☐ Concerns:

☐ Overall job satisfaction:

Need for follow-up?   ☐ No   ☐ Yes   (If so, when?) _____

Phone Interviewer _____

Date _____

SECTION
26

Job Design

Job design is an organizational process that combines a set of tasks and requirements into a job package that you can use to recruit, evaluate, and supervise volunteers. Designing a volunteer job is done before writing a job description or a task card. In this early phase, work for volunteers can come from one of three sources: (1) staff members who have a project or task, (2) potential volunteers who have a specialized skill you can use, or (3) work that needs doing badly enough to become obvious to even the casual customer.

Solid advance planning and organization are the cornerstones of a good volunteer program. Staff should understand that they can't get volunteer help immediately on demand. A staff request for volunteer help with little or no notice may go unfilled. Unless you happen to have a "general-purpose" volunteer with available time, you obviously cannot meet such requests. To avoid this problem, work with the staff to organize potential projects or tasks ahead of time.

The following are key points to consider as you begin the process of designing jobs for your volunteer program:

Task complexity and coordination;

Skill sets requirements;

Training requirements;

Time requirements; and

Legal requirements.

TASK COMPLEXITY AND COORDINATION

Tasks can range from the very simple and routine to the highly involved and complex. A single task such as clipping articles for a pamphlet file can involve hidden complexities in judgment and decision making. Merely handing a pair of scissors to a volunteer and instructing him or her to cut out articles in the newspapers that relate to local schools involves some judgment on the volunteer's part. For example, should the volunteer cut out the small article buried in the sports section on the high school wrestling meet? Should she read and mark appropriate articles first so that she does not clip out one news item only to find out she destroyed another one on the reverse side of the page? Is she expected to cite the article? How?

Even the overtly simple task of shelf maintenance can involve some judgment on the part of the volunteer. Questions such as should she shift books when a shelf is full or should large books be placed on their spines need to be addressed by staff before the volunteer actually begins to work.

A job that has many different tasks to complete may be complex but is still considered one "job" because each task is related to a specific goal. A good example is setting up a meeting room with chairs, tables, a microphone, amplifier, and a demonstration computer with a data projector. The job requires a knowledge of electrical equipment, including computers, and the physical ability to move and set up furniture according to a designated arrangement.

Conversely, a library manager wants to supervise only one volunteer. This individual will be expected to work on a data entry project, dust the bookshelves, and reshelve the magazines. The skill sets, interests, and primary responsibilities are too diverse for only one volunteer. If you did hire someone interested in all three jobs, he or she would probably prefer (and do) one task (e.g., data entry) over the others (e.g., dusting stacks) and would no doubt ignore or become sloppy in performing the less desirable work. If you pressed him or her to do all the assigned duties, the volunteer would probably quit.

Task coordination is an important element in job design. The issues here are whether the job requires working with another volunteer or staff person, or is dependent on a primary task being performed. A volunteer delivering books to homebound customers depends on a staff member to pull and check out the books to be delivered. Thus, two people have to coordinate their efforts to make the homebound program work. A volunteer who distributes program fliers at local schools is free to set her schedule as long as the flyers are handed out by a particular date. She does not need to coordinate with anyone to get her task done.

As you start reviewing task complexity and coordination requirements, be sure to write down the job specifications as you discuss them with the supervising staff member. The notes you take will become the basis for writing the job description or task card as well as recruitment flyers.

SKILL SET REQUIREMENTS

It is not uncommon for a highly experienced staff member to flippantly say, "Any dummy can do this job." Years of experience hide the skills necessary to do a task. We all tend to forget what it takes to first learn a task that we now do by rote. A volunteer who has worked in a bookstore may still have to learn to run a no-budget book sale for the library and an experienced secretary may take a while to learn a different version of software on the library computer.

As you design your jobs, you need to determine the types of skills required for the volunteer to be successful. Tasks such as repairing audiocassettes, writing promotional materials, performing online searches, or baking cookies need a certain level of skill, as does alphabetizing, following directions, understanding sequencing, and the ability to write and communicate orally.

The staff member should explain precisely what tasks are needed and how they are done. During your discussion, focus on the skill set and take notes. If you have the time, try to perform the tasks yourself. It is important to see this process as designing a complete job that you can use to recruit volunteers over a period of time. This is an important part of building a successful volunteer program.

At this stage, your notes on the complexity of the task and coordination requirements may be only a scratch list of the expected procedures to be followed and a list of skills that will be needed by a successful volunteer. Stay focused on the job's characteristics and avoid stereotyping personality characteristics and personality types for the position. By building on skill sets, you can be a better decision maker later when you have to make recommendations on the volunteers applying for the job.

TRAINING REQUIREMENTS

Training time depends on the complexity of the job defined by the expectations of the supervisor. Do not underestimate this time. For some individuals with previous experience, a few minutes of instruction and a quick demonstration are all that are necessary to get started. For example, an elementary schoolteacher volunteering to put up a bulletin board for National Library Week will likely understand the directions and intent of the supervising staff member. In this instance, you recruited an individual who is bringing job-specific training to the library. However, most new volunteers will not have the level of focused experience that may be required.

An important aspect of designing a job is taking into consideration the physical demands and training that are required to accomplish the work. Some examples of this type of training include demonstrating how to set up a foldable extension ladder, correctly pushing a cart of books from the processing workstation to the circulation desk, and lifting and carrying boxes or heavy book bags. In addition, your notes need to identify the type of equipment (e.g., stepping stools, ladders, hammers, and garden rakes) needed to complete the work.

TIME REQUIREMENTS

Is the job designed for a one-time or an ongoing project? There are volunteers who want only a short-term commitment and a one-time project fits their needs. For people who want consistency in their lives, an ongoing project is best.

Generally the time requirements are obvious from the beginning. Sometimes a short-term project is successful and the supervisor decides to continue it for an indefinite period. The volunteer recruited for the first project may have all the skills and interests, but not the commitment, for an ongoing project. The job design has to be modified to reflect the change in the program, and a new volunteer must be found to fill the position.

LEGAL REQUIREMENTS

Library policy may require that people who perform certain kinds of jobs, whether they are staff or volunteers, must meet certain legal requirements. Individuals driving vehicles for the library must produce a valid driver's license, show proof of insurance, and submit a current motor vehicle record showing their driving history. Individuals with too many points or tickets should not be accepted for this type of position. Similarly, volunteers working in the children's department, reading to children off-site, or delivering books to homebound customers may have to agree to a background check.

An important legal issue to consider is the physical demands and equipment requirements for a job. The legal question here is what must the library do to make reasonable accommodations for a volunteer who has a physical disability.

SECTION
27

Job Descriptions

A volunteer job description is a single document that combines all the pertinent information needed to perform a job. A well-written job description is the basis for recruiting, interviewing, and selecting a volunteer. It allows the volunteer to decide if she or he is interested in and willing to do the listed tasks and expectations. Finally, a job description reduces misunderstanding about a volunteer's role and encourages staff acceptance of the volunteers and your program.

When you start writing job descriptions, the following are important points to consider:

Complexity of a job description;

Integrating volunteer and staff job descriptions; and

Purpose of a job description.

COMPLEXITY OF A JOB DESCRIPTION

A written job description reorganizes your job design information into a set of titled sections. Typical section headings include job title; duties and responsibilities; time, training, and skill requirements; reporting relationships; and qualifications. Additional headings can include working conditions, physical requirements, education, and special requirements such as a driver's license.

If you review the paid staffs' job descriptions, you may find some of the aforementioned sections under the general heading of "job duties and responsibilities." For legal reasons, this section is subdivided into "essential functions" and "other duties and functions." This is done to reduce discrimination against individuals who have disabilities and can perform essential functions but not necessarily all the secondary duties and functions. Volunteer jobs do not legally require this type of breakdown; therefore, you might want to get approval on the format.

There are many ways to design and write a job description. You might want to experiment with different styles and get comments from volunteers to determine which design is the most useful and appropriate. Try to stay away from legal jargon, long, complicated sentences, and abstract descriptions. Keep it simple and to the point.

Samples 27-1–27-16 illustrate several different formats (and in addition provide you with examples of a wide range of volunteer positions). The current trend is to design job descriptions that also can be used as recruitment tools to hand out to interested individuals or placed in a display rack. In contrast, job descriptions for staff positions serve as legal documents for the library organization.

An example of a task card is found at sample 27-15. Writing a task card is a relatively quick interim step between job design notes and the final job description. If you have a volunteer position requiring an individual to sort and organize the newspapers and throw away the old issues based on a predetermined date, a task card is useful. It guides the volunteer through each step of the process. A staff supervisor uses the card to check on the progress of the work. Obviously, these cards need to be clearly written and pretested so that most volunteers can follow the steps. Having a task card does not preclude writing a job description.

INTEGRATING STAFF AND VOLUNTEER JOB DESCRIPTIONS

The volunteer job description usually contains a section on departmental relationship(s), that is, who the volunteer works with or reports to in the organization. Most of the time, the supervisor probably will not be the volunteer manager. Therefore, staff members that supervise volunteers need to have this function written into their job descriptions, thereby reducing the possibility of complaints. This integration of the supervisory function requires cooperation from the library administration or the personnel manager, who is probably responsible for updating staff job descriptions.

Examples of staff job descriptions concerning volunteer supervision appear below.

"_____ (position title) supervises the duties of library volunteers in the department, including instruction, evaluation, and recommendation for awards and recognition."

"_____ (position name) supervises department volunteers so that the library provides better service to the community."
A similar statement can be included on other staff job descriptions with the following changes: "_____ (position title, e.g., Library Assistant I) works with department volunteers to enhance service to the community."

By incorporating these statements into all staff position descriptions, you demonstrate the importance of integrating volunteers into the library system. Staff performance appraisals can reflect the degree of a person's success in directing and working with volunteers.

A staff member may ask, "Why should I work with volunteers. What is in it for me?" This is a good question. One immediate benefit is a chance to gain supervisory experience (including additional training), which is often not available to many library positions. This skill can be documented and added to the individual's personnel file. He or she can be rewarded for this activity during the performance appraisal. In addition, this skill can be added to a resume. Finally, working with volunteers from different backgrounds can bring new perspectives to one's job and a chance to meet and work with new people.

PURPOSE OF A JOB DESCRIPTION

The immediate purpose of a volunteer job description is to recruit, select, and place appropriate volunteers in jobs. Statements of "duty and responsibility" convert into good interview questions. Similarly, each qualification, skill set, and time commitment becomes a qualifying interview question. For example, the statement in the job description that requires "the ability to access and retrieve computerized information" can be rephrased in an interview. You can ask, "What experiences have you had using a computer to get information?" If the job requires the volunteer to work independently you can ask, "In which jobs or volunteer activities did you work without close supervision?"

In the section on job duties, expectations, and skills, there is an implicit set of performance standards that the volunteer is expected to meet. Phrases such as "accuracy in spelling" or the "ability to work with a minimum of supervision" assume that the volunteer can demonstrate these skills at an acceptable level of performance. The criteria for acceptable or unacceptable work are on the evaluation form, not in the job description.

Included are samples 27-1 to 27-16 to illustrate job descriptions and the range of tasks library volunteers perform.

SAMPLE 27-1
Job Description: Adopt-a-Shelf Program

Duties and Responsibilities

- On a weekly basis, accurately shelf read an assigned area of the library making corrections as necessary leaving the books in the correct order and the shelving looking neat and tidy

Job Requirements

- Must be able to work independently
- Must be accurate

Time Requirement

- A minimum of one hour a week for a minimum of three months. Amount will vary depending on the number of shelves being maintained

Training Requirements

- Orientation to the library
- Training on the Dewey Decimal System of shelving books
- Training on the application of the Dewey Decimal System to the Douglas Public Library District

Responsible to

———————————— Library Manager
and/or other designated staff

Liaison

————————————

Volunteer Services Coordinator

Duties and Responsibilities

- Using the reader profile information sheets gathered from the patrons in the Deckers area and current request forms, search the district's collection to find books, magazines, etc., to match their needs and specific requests.
- Using the library card number assigned to each individual Books-by-Mail patron, take selections to the circulation desk to have the staff check them out. Record book selections in patron files.
- Package the library selections in the assigned U.S. mailbags, address, and leave in the designated place for the volunteer driver to pick up.

Job Requirements

- Must be able to work independently.
- Be familiar with (or able to learn) the Douglas Public Library District's computerized catalog system.
- Must feel comfortable talking with patrons on the telephone concerning their reading selections, overdue books, and/or other needs.
- Must have good organizational skills.

Time Requirement

- 2-3 hours per week for a minimum of three months

Training Requirements

- Orientation to the library
- One-hour training class on the computerized catalog system (if needed)
- Training with the Books-by-Mail program coordinator

Responsible to

_____ Library Manager
and/or Books-by-Mail Coordinator

Liaison

_____

Volunteer Services Coordinator

JOB TITLE: Branch Library Volunteer

RESPONSIBLE TO: Branch Supervisor

JOB RESPONSIBILITIES: Organizing magazines and audiovisual materials, shelving books, reading shelves, etc. (whatever jobs need to be done when the volunteer is available).

TIME REQUIRED: Minimum of 1-2 hours per week

LENGTH OF COMMITMENT: Negotiable—ongoing

TRAINING PROVIDED: Orientation and instruction provided by branch Assistant.

QUALIFICATIONS, SPECIAL SKILLS REQUIRED, and RESTRICTIONS: Ability to sort materials in alphabetical and/or Dewey Decimal. Ability to access, input, and retrieve information from a computer. Ability to bend to floor level or reach a height of 75 inches. Ability to push movable carts loaded to a maximum of 250 pounds. Ability to read a minimum print size equal to elite type. Ability to tolerate dust, mold, etc. accumulated on books. Ability to lift up to 40 pounds. Knowledge of library policies and procedures.

JOB TITLE: Shelf "Reader" All Branches

RESPONSIBLE TO: Branch Head or Designated Branch Staff Person

JOB RESPONSIBILITIES: To "read" shelves by placing books in Dewey Decimal order, alphabetically by the author's name or as per collection specifies. Volunteer will be assigned sections of a center to read and straighten. Accuracy needed for this job.

TIME REQUIRED: 3 hours per week

LENGTH OF COMMITMENT: Ongoing

TRAINING PROVIDED: Orientation and instruction provided by Center Staff.

QUALIFICATIONS, SPECIAL SKILLS REQUIRED, and RESTRICTIONS: Ability to sort materials in alphabetical and/or Dewey Decimal. Ability to access, input, and retrieve information from a computer. Ability to bend to floor level or reach a height of 75 inches. Ability to read a minimum print size equal to elite type. Ability to tolerate dust, mold, etc., accumulated on books. Ability to lift up to 40 pounds. Knowledge of library policies and procedures.

JOB TITLE: Branch Library Storytellers

RESPONSIBLE TO: Branch Supervisor

JOB RESPONSIBILITIES: Read stories, play games, and do simple craft projects for children attending story hours at branch libraries.

TIME REQUIRED: 1 hour per week (Plus setup time)

LENGTH OF COMMITMENT: 3-6 months

TRAINING PROVIDED: Orientation and instruction provided by Branch Staff (volunteer will read from preselected kits which include stories, finger plays, crafts, and film-strips).

QUALIFICATIONS, SPECIAL SKILLS REQUIRED, and RESTRICTIONS: Ability to work with preschool children, good voice for reading to children. Flexible personality and creative traits desirable. Must be dependable. Ability to read a minimum print size equal to elite type. Ability to tolerate dust, mold, etc., accumulated on books. Ability to lift up to 40 pounds. Knowledge of library policies and procedures.

JOB TITLE: Children's Center, Miscellaneous Volunteer

RESPONSIBLE TO: Center Head or Designated Center Staff

JOB RESPONSIBILITIES: Sort book shelves and carts; check media for damages, label and replace bags for media materials; put filmstrips and tapes in alphabetical order; straighten book shelves; put chairs away; prepare crafts; do book jackets; stamp withdrawn books; straighten magazines; pick up books; read bins; sharpen pencils and replace paper at computer stations.

TIME REQUIRED: 3 hours per week

LENGTH OF COMMITMENT: Ongoing

TRAINING PROVIDED: Orientation and instruction provided by Center Staff

QUALIFICATIONS, SPECIAL SKILLS REQUIRED, and RESTRICTIONS: Ability to work with pre-school children, flexibility in schedule, attention to detail. Ability to sort materials in alphabetical and/or Dewey Decimal. Ability to access, input, and retrieve information from a computer. Ability to bend to floor level or reach a height of 75 inches. Ability to push movable carts loaded to a maximum of 250 pounds. Ability to read a minimum print size equal to elite type. Ability to tolerate dust, mold, etc., accumulated on books. Ability to lift up to 40 pounds. Knowledge of library policies and procedures.

JOB TITLE: Book Bazaar Volunteer

RESPONSIBLE TO: Library Director and/or XiBeta coordinator

JOB RESPONSIBILITIES: Set up, sell, or tear down of annual event. Event held in mid-spring to benefit the library and XiBeta. Requires 1 to 2 days setup/organization of donated books and ongoing straightening of sale tables and tear down.

TIME REQUIRED: Event lasts 4 to 5 days, 4 to 12 hours per day . . . as much as possible.

LENGTH OF COMMITMENT: As the volunteer is able

TRAINING PROVIDED: Orientation and training by XiBeta coordinator.

QUALIFICATIONS, SPECIAL SKILLS REQUIRED, and RESTRICTIONS: Person with enough strength to lift boxes of books for the setup period. For straightening, one needs to be able to stand on a cement floor and lift books and straighten the tables. A basic knowledge of fiction vs. mystery vs. romance books is helpful for sorting. Ability to bend to floor level or reach a height of 75 inches. Ability to push movable carts loaded to a maximum of 250 pounds. Ability to read a minimum print size equal to elite type. Ability to tolerate dust, mold, etc., accumulated on books. Ability to lift up to 40 pounds.

SAMPLE 27-8
Job Description: Children's Center, Summer Reading/Game Volunteer and Shelver

JOB TITLE: Children's Center, Summer Reading/Game Volunteer and Shelver

RESPONSIBLE TO: Center Head or Designated Center Staff

JOB RESPONSIBILITIES: Understands the way the Summer Reading Program works and explains it simply to children. Aids children in moving across the "game" board in understanding other special features regarding the game. Shelves returned books.

TIME REQUIRED: 2-4 hours per week

LENGTH OF COMMITMENT: 2 months in summer

TRAINING PROVIDED: Orientation and instructions provided by Center Staff.

QUALIFICATIONS, SPECIAL SKILLS REQUIRED, and RESTRICTIONS: Ability to work with pre-school children; flexibility in schedule and attention to detail. Ability to sort materials in alphabetical and/or Dewey Decimal. Ability to bend to floor level or reach a height of 75 inches. Ability to push movable carts loaded to a maximum of 250 pounds. Ability to read a minimum print size equal to elite type. Ability to tolerate dust, mold, etc., accumulated on books. Ability to lift up to 40 pounds. Knowledge of library policies and procedures.

JOB TITLE: Children's Center, Graphics Volunteer

RESPONSIBLE TO: Center Head or Designated Center Staff

JOB RESPONSIBILITIES: Assist with Summer Reading Program bulletin board, crafts, and other bulletin board displays and book exhibits.

TIME REQUIRED: Be on call for summer reading projects, which will involve varying time requests.

LENGTH OF COMMITMENT: Ongoing

TRAINING PROVIDED: Orientation and instructions provided by Center Staff.

QUALIFICATIONS, SPECIAL SKILLS REQUIRED, and RESTRICTIONS: Enjoy graphic arts/crafts; be creative and be able to work a flexible schedule. Ability to bend to floor level or reach a height of 75 inches. Ability to read a minimum print size equal to elite type. Ability to tolerate dust, mold, etc., accumulated on books. Ability to lift up to 40 pounds. Knowledge of library policies and procedures.

JOB TITLE: Periodicals Volunteer

RESPONSIBLE TO: Popular Materials Designated Center Staff

JOB RESPONSIBILITIES: To shelf-read periodicals; to reshelve/organize magazines; to relabel magazine containers; to help maintain order in periodical area and possible computer input.

TIME REQUIRED: 2-4 hours per week

LENGTH OF COMMITMENT: 3-6 months—ongoing

TRAINING PROVIDED: Training on MCPLD's periodical organization system and rationale and computer training as needed.

QUALIFICATIONS, SPECIAL SKILLS REQUIRED, and RESTRICTIONS: Ability to access, input, and retrieve information from a computer. Ability to bend to floor level or reach a height of 75 inches. Ability to read a minimum print size equal to elite type. Ability to lift up to 40 pounds. Accuracy in spelling, alphabetizing, and a penchant for neatness!

SAMPLE 27-11
Job Description: Clerk

JOB TITLE: Clerk—All Centers

RESPONSIBLE TO: Center Head or Designated Center Staff

JOB RESPONSIBILITIES: Works with book orders. Alphabetizes, types, or word processes special lists. Types and replaces labels and color coding tape as needed. Adds records to Center database on PC. Assists in processing withdrawn materials. Photocopies, types, files, and does other clerical tasks (as needed).

TIME REQUIRED: Minimum of 3 hours per week

LENGTH OF COMMITMENT: Minimum of 21 hours

TRAINING PROVIDED: Orientation and instructions provided by Center Staff.

QUALIFICATIONS, SPECIAL SKILLS REQUIRED, and RESTRICTIONS: Ability to sort and organize materials in alphabetical and/or Dewey decimal order; types and/or has personal computer skills. Ability to bend to floor level or reach a height of 75 inches. Ability to read a minimum print size equal to elite type. Ability to tolerate dust, mold, etc., accumulated on books and materials. Ability to lift up to 40 pounds. Skill in operation of office machines and equipment. Knowledge of library automation.

SAMPLE 27-12
Job Description: Shelver

JOB TITLE: Shelver

RESPONSIBLE TO: Center Head or Designated Center Staff

JOB RESPONSIBILITIES: Sort, shelve, or file library materials, books, magazines, newspapers, discs, tapes, AV materials, microforms, and other media.

TIME REQUIRED: Minimum of 3 hours per week

LENGTH OF COMMITMENT: Minimum of 3 months—ongoing

TRAINING PROVIDED: Orientation by volunteer coordinator and instruction in appropriate system by designated center staff.

QUALIFICATIONS, SPECIAL SKILLS REQUIRED, and RESTRICTIONS: Ability to bend to floor level or reach a height of 75 inches. Ability to push movable carts loaded to a maximum of 250 pounds. Ability to read minimum print size equal to elite type. Ability to tolerate dust, mold, etc., accumulated on books and materials. Ability to lift up to 40 pounds. Skill in operation of office machines and equipment. Knowledge of library automation system.

JOB TITLE: Reference Updater and Filer

RESPONSIBLE TO: Reference Center Head or Designated Center Staff

JOB RESPONSIBILITIES: Update and file reference materials; work with bibliographies; file pamphlet materials; file and work with government documents.

TIME REQUIRED: Varies with volunteer

LENGTH OF COMMITMENT: Ongoing

TRAINING PROVIDED: Orientation and instruction provided by designated Center Staff.

QUALIFICATIONS, SPECIAL SKILLS REQUIRED, and RESTRICTIONS: Dependability and good vision. Ability to access, input, and retrieve information from a computer. Ability to bend to floor level or reach a height of 75 inches. Ability to read a minimum print size equal to elite type. Ability to tolerate dust, mold, etc., accumulated on books and materials. Ability to lift up to 40 pounds. Skill in operation of office machines and equipment. Knowledge of library automation system.

JOB TITLE: Book Menders

RESPONSIBLE TO: Check-out Supervisor

JOB RESPONSIBILITIES: Mend those books which need not be sent to the professional binder and maintain an inventory of mending supplies.

TIME REQUIRED: Minimum 3-4 hours per week

LENGTH OF COMMITMENT: 6 months

TRAINING PROVIDED: Orientation by Volunteer Coordinator. Mending procedures and instruction by staff personnel and current experienced menders.

QUALIFICATIONS, SPECIAL SKILLS REQUIRED, and RESTRICTIONS: Ability to lift up to 40 pounds. Ability to tolerate dust, mold, glues, and compounds associated with the task. Ability to read a minimum print size equal to elite type. Special interest in book restoration.

RESPONSIBLE TO: Center Head or Designated Staff

JOB RESPONSIBILITIES: Maintenance and shelf-reading of the cassette racks. Color coding of cassettes and bags. Some data entry and special projects dealing with audiovisual.

TIME REQUIRED: 3 hours per week

LENGTH OF COMMITMENT: Ongoing

TRAINING PROVIDED: Orientation and instruction provided by designated Center Staff.

QUALIFICATIONS, SPECIAL SKILLS REQUIRED, and RESTRICTIONS: Ability to sort materials in alphabetical and/or Dewey Decimal. Ability to access, input, and retrieve information from a computer. Ability to bend to floor level or reach a height of 75 inches. Ability to push movable carts loaded to a maximum of 150 pounds. Ability to read a minimum print size equal to elite type. Ability to tolerate dust, mold, etc., accumulated on books. Ability to lift up to 40 pounds. Ability to read a minimum print size equal to elite type. Knowledge of library policies.

Task Card: Shelf Grooming

1. Your job is to spend thirty minutes grooming one section of shelving. Each shelf is numbered. To determine where to begin, you must first check the "Shelf Grooming Log" located on a clipboard in the large volunteer box.

2. To groom, you first push all of the books to the far left and adjust the bookend to hold them.

3. Make sure that all books are standing upright and not leaning.

4. Make sure that each book is even with the edge of the shelf.

5. Any oversized book that is too large for the shelf should be laid flat on the bottom shelf with its spine label facing outward.

6. Make sure to leave the section looking neat and tidy.

   We systematically go through three main areas of our collection on a rotating basis. The three main areas are:

Orange dots:	Adult Nonfiction and Biography	Shelf #1 – 668
Green Glow dots:	Adult Fiction and Large Type	Shelf #1 – 488
Yellow dots:	Juvenile and Easy Readers	Shelf #1 – 207

7. Record where you left off on the Shelf Grooming Log.

Duties and Responsibilities

- Read aloud to senior citizens housed in assisted living homes or care centers on a weekly basis.
- Select appropriate reading selections from library collection or if desired have the library staff make the selections.
- Record volunteer hours on the volunteer time sheet.
- Meet informally with staff supervisor or library manager on a regular basis to provide program feedback (at least once every three months).

Job Requirements

- Must be dependable.
- Must provide own, reliable transportation.
- Must have a love of reading, a clear loud reading voice, and a desire to share with seniors who are often no longer able to read on their own.
- Must meet the expectations of the seniors.

Time Requirements

- Must be able to commit to one hour a week for a minimum of three months.

Training Requirements

- Orientation training to the library.
- Orientation to Senior's program.

Responsible to

Philip S. Miller Library Manager
and/or

Senior Outreach Services

Liaison

Volunteer Service Coordinator
Douglas Public Library District

SECTION

28

Volunteer Recognition Policies

Volunteers like to receive some form of recognition for their contributions to your library. However, many libraries have no budget or at best a very limited budget to sponsor a formal volunteer recognition program. How then do you say thank-you to your volunteers for the work they do for the library? To begin, it is a good idea to write out a recognition policy that addresses the following points:

Formality of a recognition program;

Criteria for recognition;

Selection of outstanding volunteers;

Involvement of paid staff;

Budget;

Public awareness of recognition program; and

Staff members as volunteers.

FORMALITY OF A RECOGNITION PROGRAM

It is important to think through your recognition policies and get comments from administration and staff as you begin to develop them. These policies need to be flexible to accommodate the diversity of your volunteers. They also need to be written clearly so that you can articulate them to volunteers, administrators, and potential donors.

Recognition must be given consistently to everyone in your program, or you can create tension and conflict even with the best intentions. For example, if one volunteer receives a verbal thank-you and another is ignored, or one receives a small gift and someone else a certificate of appreciation, you may find increased dissatisfaction as an unintended consequence.

The forms of recognition do not have to be the same for everyone, but you need to be consistent within each volunteer category. For instance, young volunteers appreciate a pizza party and a certificate at an informal gathering. On the other hand, some seniors do not want to venture out at night for a program but might enjoy a noontime luncheon.

Obviously, all library volunteers can be given informal verbal recognition, even if they are in your library for court-ordered restitution. It does not take much to tell a volunteer mending books that she or he is doing a great job. Similarly, volunteers using the library as a way to earn service credits can be given recognition with a note on their sign-off form or a separate letter of thank-you. People remember these comments. In this regard, your recognition policy can include a statement that supervising staff will make an effort to acknowledge good volunteer work.

CRITERIA FOR RECOGNITION

On what basis do you want to give formal recognition? Some options include:

Number of hours worked in a given time period, such as six months or a year;

Lifetime volunteer hours;

Number of months volunteering for the library, regardless of the hours contributed;

Completion or management of an important project;

Measurable accomplishments such as the number of telephone calls made, the number of books mended, dollars collected during a fund-raising campaign, and so forth; and

Recommendations by key staff members.

From a policy point of view, you need to consider whether you will award volunteers based on one of these criteria or several, and if the recipients will receive the same kind of recognition awards. Do you want your volunteers to perceive the awards as having the same or different value? If everyone, regardless of category, receives the same colored certificate, the perceived recognition is seen as equal. If some people receive a plaque and others receive a certificate, then you are clearly differentiating by the type of awards. In like manner, do you want to build on the same award every year? For example, you can award pins the first year and then add a bar for every year of additional service rendered.

A second policy issue is whether to honor past achievements, current activities, or both. Hence, do you invite only those volunteers who worked a set number of hours over the past year, even if they are no longer active, or do you limit your invitations to those currently active who worked the requisite number of hours? Will you invite all currently active volunteers, even those who are new to the volunteer recognition event? Good arguments can be made on both sides of these issues, and the size of your volunteer group may force you to choose an option based on room size, costs, or other administrative considerations.

SELECTION OF OUTSTANDING VOLUNTEERS

An important step in the recognition process is to decide if you want to select a single "volunteer of the year" for the entire system, for each branch, or for a category of volunteer (seniors, youth, etc.). Conversely, do you want to recognize the contributions of all volunteers equally? These are important issues.

Choosing the specific criteria can be a challenge. If you use only the number of hours volunteered, then the majority of volunteers are out of luck. If you use a criterion such as the degree of dedication, you have to carefully decide how to measure this so that others perceive the selection as fair. If you use a committee, who will select the committee members and what criteria will they use to make the recommendation?

A final policy issue to consider is whether an individual can be a "volunteer of the year" only once or can he or she be selected again? If you decide there is no limit, then how do you address the issue of fairness and objectivity? As you make your final decision, it is a good idea to get comments from the library staff, including volunteers.

INVOLVEMENT OF PAID STAFF

How should you involve paid staff in your volunteer recognition event? Do you want to give a "volunteer supervisor of the year" award to a staff member who is successful working with volunteers? Are there staff members who deserve special recognition for supporting volunteers and your program? This is both a policy and a financial issue. On the policy side of the equation is the integration of paid staff, especially those working with volunteers and library volunteers receiving the awards. By integrating both in the same event, you can develop a feeling of partnership as both groups see themselves as a part of the whole library team.

BUDGET

A large party with library personnel and volunteers can be costly. The more people and the more food, the more complicated the event. Hidden costs will come up and allowances must be made for these. If you, a volunteer, or a member of the staff is creative at fund-raising, now is the time to ask for help. Many local businesses might be willing to donate or discount food, gifts, or certificates for this event. The balancing act occurs between your recognition policies and the amount of funds available. For example, you may want supervising staff present, unless there are too many volunteers and guests, and your budget is limited. You may have to invite volunteers receiving awards and one guest.

Here is another important policy issue. Will your library support the use of taxpayer funds for recognition events for staff or volunteers? Some libraries do not see this as a problem. Others view it as a potential public relations issue, especially in tight budget times. It is important to discuss this with the administration before any event is planned. Keep in mind that the library position on this matter may shift over time.

Underscoring your recognition policies must be the intent to see the event as a sincere thank-you from the library community. The sincerity of the volunteer recognition is not dependent on or measured by the funds available or the number of people invited. When your volunteers go home after a successful event, what they will remember is the way you and the staff showed honest appreciation for the work that they did for the library. The small gifts, certificates, and awards may be stored, but the feelings they hold will linger. Your goal is to reinforce a feeling of commitment for library volunteering.

PUBLIC AWARENESS OF VOLUNTEER RECOGNITION

Decide to what degree you want your recognition event to be an internal affair versus a community or public relations event. You can make a good case for either side. If you have volunteers who are easily embarrassed or who are uncomfortable in the limelight, a small internal event is less stressful for them. Alternatively, free advertising generated by an article on an annual recognition event for the library volunteers is a good way to get the word out about your program. Using this rationale, the more people who know about your program, the better the chance of attracting volunteers with a wide range of skills and aptitudes.

Remember that once you choose a direction, it is not irreversible. As with all policies, you will need to review it periodically to make sure that earlier decisions still make sense considering changes within your library, your volunteer program, and the local community.

Volunteer Recognition Policy Statements

In appreciation of our volunteers' contributions of time and skills, the library will provide a yearly recognition event and adequate funding for the purchase of special awards and recognition gifts for all volunteers.

The library will formally recognize outstanding volunteer(s) of the year as voted on by staff members that work with them.

The library will recognize outstanding volunteers from all branches based on the number of hours contributed over the past year.

Community volunteers who provide more than five hundred hours of service to the library will have their names placed on a volunteer plaque.

Library trustees are recognized as important community volunteers who give their time freely to act as advocates for library services within our community.

The staff is encouraged to give informal thank-yous to our community volunteers as an acknowledgment of their many services to the library.

Young volunteers will be rewarded on a periodic basis for the services they provide to our library.

The library encourages staff members who regularly work with volunteers to attend the annual volunteer reception.

The library will honor one volunteer supervisor of the year with an award at the volunteer appreciation event.

Recognition Programs

As you begin to think about types of recognition programs, consider the following points:

Informal recognition;

Informal affairs;

Organizing formal affairs; and

Evaluation of recognition programs.

INFORMAL RECOGNITION

A recognition program is as simple as verbal comments of praise. Therefore, your decision to be consistent in passing on positive comments from supervisors to a volunteer is one of the strongest forms of recognition, especially for a library with a limited budget. You let the volunteer know she or he is a contributing member of the team by simply saying that you heard great things about his or her work. A thank-you card or note from you or the supervisor also goes a long way toward recognizing a volunteer's time and effort. The cost to buy note cards is minimal but the impact is significant.

INFORMAL AFFAIRS

Slightly more formal than verbal or written recognition is a morning breakfast or coffee, a brunch, or a casual potluck luncheon. At these events you recognize and say thank-you to the volunteer group as well as to the individual volunteer.

These informal affairs are a form of peer recognition and encourage the individual's commitment to the library volunteer program.

There are other times when informal events are appropriate and meaningful, such as a milestone (a birthday, achieving five hundred volunteer hours, or completing specialized training). You can make these occasions extraordinary by inviting volunteers and staff to the celebration.

ORGANIZING FORMAL AFFAIRS

At the other end of the spectrum is a major affair with local dignitaries, formal presentations, and possibly the media. Formalizing the recognition program requires funds and advance preparation time to make the event successful (see sample 29-1). The basic structure of these affairs is well defined, but the variations are almost endless. A typical outline for a formal recognition event is:

Key introductions;

Awards and gifts;

Special acknowledgments;

Closing comments; and

Social time with food and beverages.

These events can be held in the late afternoon, evening, or on a weekend morning when guests can attend. You can plan the program to coincide with national library week to bring special attention to the library. Good alternative times are early spring (February or March) and fall (October or November) when there are fewer holidays and less vacation travel.

The planning period begins a few months in advance to schedule a room, choose a theme, design invitations, invite dignitaries, print certificates, acquire awards, gifts, and prizes, and order or coordinate the food. This is usually the biggest volunteer event of the year. Even so, it is not likely that library staff will be assigned to work with you. However, you can draw on the interests and skills of your volunteers to help make this a festive occasion.

The challenge in organizing a formal event is your ability to keep it from becoming stuffy and obligatory. You want it to be enjoyable, lively, and desirable for each volunteer and his or her guest so that they will want to attend. However, you may find that some volunteers will not come because they view their work as a quiet service to the community. Others may not feel comfortable in a large group of people. It is still important to acknowledge their work and contribution at this time.

EVALUATION OF RECOGNITION PROGRAMS

Evaluating your recognition program does not mean adding up financial costs or attempting to get more funds into your budget. Rather, it means asking the basic question, "Am I giving sincere thanks and recognition to the library volunteers?"

It is a good idea to do a "reality check" on how you and the staff are recognizing volunteers throughout the year. This includes both informal and formal recognition programs. Have you given a verbal or written thank-you to your volunteers at least once during the year? Do you know if the supervising staff recognized their volunteers? In which way? How many informal affairs did you sponsor over the past year? Did you get representative opinions, both good and bad, on any formal events that you organized? What would you do differently next year?

For small- and medium-sized libraries, volunteer comments do not have to mean a large-scale survey on your part. Throughout the year, you can ask volunteers how they feel about working at the library and what they would like to see in the way of a thank-you. If a volunteer does not feel appreciated, his or her response to this question will be different from one who does.

1. Identify respective/active volunteers in each area of library service.

   - bookmobile
   - friends
   - homebound
   - library
   - library board

2. Develop a list of those businesses that have donated or have helped the library in the designated year.

3. Check lists from #1 and #2 above against lists from previous year to make certain that no one is overlooked.

4. Ask that designated members of friends and others who have worked with volunteers review the lists (#1 and #2) to see that no one is overlooked.

5. Write to the local supermarkets and ask them to donate gift certificates for food at the awards program.

6. Send appropriate invitations to those ID'd in the lists above.

7. Develop a program list of names with area(s) of service indicated.

8. Proof spelling of all names.

9. Develop an awards committee to plan and implement the volunteer awards program and select the outstanding volunteer(s).

   - speak with local florists about donating a floral arrangement
   - complete the city's room setup form
   - order food and beverages

10. Obtain a new guest book for those attending to sign.

11. Obtain name tags for volunteers to wear while at the reception.

12. Obtain $25 gift certificates for the outstanding volunteers.

13. Get a price sheet for advertising in the local newspaper and give this information to the library director. To be used to list the honored volunteers.

**Have a Great Volunteer Reception
and Start Planning for the Next Reception!**

SECTION
30

Awards, Gifts, and Perks

What types of recognition items can you give to volunteers that are affordable and meaningfully tied to the program? This is a difficult question to answer. Awards are presented for accomplishments, gifts are given for volunteering one's time, and perks can be used for either purpose. Usually, what is important is not what you give to a volunteer, but the thought behind it. In this section, we will look at recognition, especially on a limited budget.

RECOGNITION BUDGET

For many small- to medium-sized libraries, the volunteer budget for awards or gifts will be nonexistent or small. The amount available to spend per person may be less than $5. Based on your policies, you need to decide whether a few people will receive awards or everyone will be recognized. If you present a recognition award to everyone, then you need to decide how much you can afford to spend and what you can purchase for that amount. Presenting one individual with an engraved plaque for $35 may have to be offset by giving the others printed certificates of appreciation. Alternatively, a special commendation presented by the library director to each volunteer may take more time to organize, but there is no cost involved. Creative brainstorming can give you additional ideas. There are also commercial volunteer catalog companies that provide a variety of awards and gifts in different price ranges.

One option for libraries with limited or nonexistent budgets is to seek donations from local businesses. You can do this yourself or recruit a volunteer. To begin, write a sample letter that you can use to initiate the contact, then make a list of potential donors (call each business first to find out the name of the contact person). If you start a few months before the event, you will probably receive more donations than if you start a month or two before you actually need the items. You need to accept rejection (don't take it personally) and move on to the next company. Be sure to write a thank-you letter to the donor.

If you do not have a policy, you can write a set of guidelines on acceptable donations. For example, will you take a $20 gift certificate from an adult bookstore? What will you do with gifts after the program or when donations of merchandise are not appropriate?

Finally, a small library with no budget can serve a potluck dinner provided by the staff and present small donated gifts. This type of recognition event is as much fun as an elaborate program. Everyone is pitching in to recognize and honor their volunteers.

AWARDS

Certain items by their nature are not gifts, but awards. Included in this category are certificates, plaques, written commendations, proclamations, and special logo pins. To receive one of these items, a volunteer has to earn it. The fact that a volunteer has to earn these items does not mean that you will not have an individual intentionally working to receive an award.

Almost any object can be converted into an award simply by placing an inscription on it. Thus a small glass globe of the earth becomes an award by adding the words, "In recognition for 10 years of service." Its value to the volunteer is tied to the social occasion and how it is presented. The globe given to a volunteer in your office becomes a nice paperweight, but presented by the library direc-tor or the president of the library trustees at a reception, it becomes an object of prestige and honor.

Finding awards that relate to libraries, books, or reading can be a challenge. Engraved book-marks, letter openers, library note cards, or books have been used successfully in the past. A book-plate inscribed with the volunteer's name and placed in a newly purchased book makes a long-lasting and meaningful award.

Even when some engraved plaques and tro-phies cost under $10, the costs can add up when you have several awards to present. As an alterna-tive, you can invest in one large wall plaque and add volunteer names as they reach a predeter-mined number of donated hours.

GIFTS AND PRIZES

The category of gifts and prizes relates to a person's status as a volunteer rather than to a par-ticular accomplishment. Gifts can include actual objects or gifts certificates. Based on your recog-nition policy and budget, you can give everyone a small gift or hand them out as door prizes. Any decision you make can be successful if done with a sense of respect for the volunteers and as part of an enjoyable activity. Attaching a personal thank-you card to each gift increases its value.

There is a wide variety of small thank-you gifts available. In addition to getting ideas from cre-ative volunteers and staff, you can also go through gift catalogs. Think about seeking donations from local merchants such as gift certificates from grocery stores, hotels, restaurants, movie theaters, museums, zoos, and recreational centers or amusement parks. Also, try to get donated tickets to cultural programs, community festivals, or any library-sponsored events.

Small and inexpensive gifts include baskets of candy, flowering plants, posters, balloons, spe-cialty buttons, individual pictures taken at the library, stationery, note cards, and decorative ceramic appreciation plates.

Common library theme gifts include logo T-shirts, sweaters, and sweatshirts; volunteer pins, mugs, and pens; and bookmarks and posters. Larger libraries can give certificates for merchan-dise at their gift shops. Finally, computer-generated bookmarks, note pads, funny cards, and similar items make inexpensive gifts you can give year-round.

As with most gifts, the dollar value is often less important than the spirit in which the gift is given. The gifts are merely the symbols of your recognition and thanks.

VOLUNTEER PERKS

The term *perk* is the abbreviation for *perquisite* and refers to the benefits and privileges a person receives for being a library volunteer. Perks make a job interesting and can add to the appeal of working in a library. There are two issues that need to be examined before you decide to implement any perks for the volunteers in your program. The first is whether the volunteers should receive the same perks as staff. The perk serves as a status function in many organizations. If the staff perceives that their perks are diluted because volunteers are also getting them, petty conflict can result. For example, if waiving overdue fines is a staff perk, then do you want to waive them for volunteers as well, and if you do, will there be ramifications?

A second area of concern is establishing criteria necessary to be eligible for different perks. For example, can volunteers receive perks the first day they start, or should they work a set number of hours? Can they be eligible for parking privileges after one month and waiving overdue fines after six months?

Library volunteers can receive any number of perks. Examples can range from free skills training either through class or on-the-job training to ordering a book at the staff discount. For a volunteer with artistic skills or computer graphics knowledge, designing library posters, announcements, and so forth might be considered a perk. The volunteer can also take federal and state charitable tax deductions for unpaid expenditures while volunteering. This includes automobile mileage, bus fares, and parking costs. For some volunteers looking for work experience, a job recommendation is the most important perk he or she can receive from the library.

Awards, gifts, and perks are an important part of any job. Whether or not they are tangible items, some form of recognition is essential to good management practice. Showing appreciation for the work done encourages volunteers to continue to provide their time and services to the library.

PART V

VOLUNTEER RULES AND DISCIPLINE

SECTION

31

Library Volunteer Rules

Library volunteers want and need guidance. Some staff members hesitate to enforce library rules with a volunteer, yet they need to know what the work rules are so they can feel comfortable fitting in with the staff and the ongoing library operations.

From a manager's point of view, the volunteer work rules provide clarification for which activities are acceptable, and a basis for enforcing them if necessary. For example, is a volunteer breaking a rule when she puts her lunch in the refrigerator marked "staff only"? Is the refrigerator available for use by both staff and volunteers? As volunteer managers know or find out quickly, no issue is too small to be blown out of proportion. In writing the rules or guidelines, the following are important points to cover.

Rules in the volunteer handbook;

Statement and clarification of the rules;

Unique situations; and

Enforcement policies.

RULES IN THE VOLUNTEER HANDBOOK

A volunteer handbook often evolves from a single handout that is based on the library's policies and procedures manual. A good handbook will emphasize the positive aspects of volunteering and provide a positive spin to the volunteer rules by using less formal terms such as "guidelines," "code of conduct," or "library expectations."

It is important to distinguish between general library policy rules and specific work rules. Library policy rules are broad categories of rules that affect and cover all areas of library operations. These can be written under the heading "library expectations" as exemplified in the phrase, "Library staff and volunteers are expected to." Many of these policy rules can be taken directly from the staff handbook and then reworded for your volunteer manual.

For instance, your library policy on sexual harassment describes inappropriate behaviors toward staff, volunteers, and customers. Similarly, a policy rule stating that the library is a nonsmoking workplace means that no one can smoke within the building. Other policy rules include:

Drugs and alcohol;

Customer confidentiality and privacy; and

Volunteer communications (e.g., schedule postings, bulletin boards, and e-mail content).

Work rules are more specific and pertain to behaviors such as dress codes, use of the telephones and lockers, break times, and so forth. Your volunteer handbook may state that a volunteer must be dressed appropriately to maintain the professional environment of the library. This broad rule can imply that cut-offs, short shorts, very short dresses, halter tops, or torn jeans cannot be worn to work. You probably do not want to write this list out in your handbook, but rather let staff supervisors interpret what is meant by "appropriate dress." Accordingly, a volunteer sorting donated books in the workroom should not dress the same way as a circulation clerk or page working with the public. When you work with young adult volunteers, you may find it useful to have a one-page handout that specifically states what is appropriate to wear as a volunteer and reinforce it by telling volunteers when they are not dressed appropriately.

When writing your handbook, you need to decide on the general work rules or guidelines that all volunteers must follow regardless of their assignments, and which rules are specific to departments and should be explained by the supervising staff member. A general volunteer rule is "all volunteers are expected to show up for their shift or call their staff supervisor if they are going to be late or absent." A specific department rule is "a volunteer cannot use the circulation phone to make personal calls unless there is an emergency." In another department, it is all right for either staff or volunteers to use the telephone.

Throughout the library system, you may not know the specific differences in library rules and department or branch interpretations. It is important that you decide how this information is going to be communicated and who will be responsible for conveying the information. These procedures should be spelled out before placing a volunteer to reduce the possibility of embarrassment, hurt feelings, or staff-volunteer conflicts.

Finally, you need to decide if you want the volunteer handbook to serve as a recruitment and marketing tool or a rule book. In the former case, the emphasis is on the enjoyment of volunteering and the kinds of opportunities that are available. In the latter case, the handbook is a list of work-related "do's" and "don'ts."

STATEMENT AND CLARIFICATION OF THE RULES

Ideally, the staff supervisor will take the time with the volunteer to clarify the department rules. In a busy library this may not be feasible. If there is a positively written, one- to two-page list of rules, this can supplement and highlight a verbal explanation (see sample 31-1). In either case, you need to include some or all of the following points in your list or discussion:

- Departmental dress code;
- Lockers or storage space for personal effects;
- Attendance, tardiness, or absences;
- Designated smoking areas;
- Parking;
- Telephone, fax, and copier use;

The following guidelines and procedures outline the essential expectations of your volunteer position. Please become thoroughly familiar with these expectations and be sure they are acceptable to you before making your decision to volunteer for the library.

1. Library user requests are always handled by paid library staff. Because of liability issues and because library staff are updated regularly on changes in our operations, we ask that volunteers refer all user inquiries to library staff without exception.

2. Privacy of library users' records is protected by Colorado state law. This means that you may not share any knowledge you may gain through your volunteer duties at the library of any record or other information which identifies a person as having used the library or requested or obtained specific materials or services at the library. To violate user privacy is to violate state law and is punishable by state law.

3. Volunteers and staff are expected to present a clean and neat appearance while on the job. Please dress comfortably but appropriately for your assigned task.

4. You will report to a designated staff person in the center or branch where you are volunteering and training is provided for all tasks performed. That staff person will issue you a locker for your valuables and a volunteer badge for identification. Please be sure to always use your locker and wear your badge. When questions arise, please feel free to ask the designated staff person for further clarification.

5. Your volunteer time is an integral part of the coordination of staff hours and duties. If you are unable to come in at your scheduled time, please call your designated staff person or the center.

6. Be sure to sign in and out every day you are volunteering. Volunteer hour tabulation is an important part of the library's statistics.

7. Parking for main branch volunteers is in the public parking lot.

8. At the main branch, volunteers are invited to enjoy their breaks in the lounge at the back of the reference center. You may store your own cup in the cupboards if you wish. Please store all food and unsealed beverages in the break room and wash and put away any dishes you use.

9. If you have any comments or concerns not addressed by your designated staff person or center manager, please contact the community relations manager who is here for you!

- Office supplies;
- Reporting injuries;
- Break times and break areas; and
- Holiday schedules and library closures.

Most people do not read lists of rules, and when they do, they usually interpret them in terms of their own prior experiences. Volunteers do not know how specific rules are applied in the library. For example, a volunteer can read from a list of rules that telephones are not to be used for personal reasons unless in an emergency. In their prior work or volunteer experiences, similar rules were not enforced. Therefore, the volunteer operating on past experiences may proceed to make personal or business calls. At this point, rule clarification is important and a face-to-face explanation is required.

Who is responsible for clarifying and enforcing the rules? If you are in a large library or one with several branches, you are not in a position to enforce the rules yourself. If you have an orientation program, this is the time to clarify the rules. Enforcement needs be the role of the supervising staff members. However, some have limited supervisory experience and find it awkward to tell a volunteer to follow a rule. Therefore, you might hear from a secondhand source that a volunteer is breaking a rule. Now you are expected to act. If this is the case, you need to become a "fact finder" by either observing the rule violation yourself or asking questions to determine the veracity of the statements. You can take action only after you have verified all the facts.

UNIQUE SITUATIONS

All rules include gray areas that make it unclear how to proceed under certain circumstances. A large part of any volunteer manager's job is interpreting ambiguous situations. Consider the example of a volunteer who gives the library telephone number to her elderly mother so her mother can call her if it becomes necessary. The staff complains that the volunteer is receiving too many personal calls during her shift. The volunteer claims she receives only one or two calls at the most from her mother. However, she observes that certain employees are receiving personal calls from their children and other family members. What can you do to defuse this situation?

There are no set rules that cover all contingencies. At times you will need to interpret the rules as they apply to specific situations. In the example above, if the staff is allowed to receive personal calls, can the department rules be stretched to cover volunteers? Can you have the volunteer keep track of the number of calls she receives per shift for a couple of weeks to determine the number of calls? Can you limit the incoming calls to two per shift? Each question offers several options that must be considered in light of either setting a poor precedent or being too rigid to deal with unique volunteer concerns.

Library policies and rules can change over time due to evolving circumstances or at the discretion of the library director. Be sure to state this somewhere in your volunteer handbook. In this way, you protect the library organization and managers when they have to make changes that affect volunteers.

ENFORCEMENT POLICIES

It is important to remember that most volunteers want to be effective at their jobs and follow library rules. Any enforcement is usually focused on additional clarification or the consequences of not following a rule. For example, you are told a volunteer is frequently using the fax machine for personal work. You or the immediate supervisor needs to explain that this ties up the fax machine for library-related business. Luckily, most volunteers will gladly change their behavior to accommodate the library. However, it is the habitual violator that creates the problem. A problem volunteer may say, for example, "I'm not using the fax machine any more than anyone else. I'm being singled out because the staff doesn't want me to volunteer here!" In this situation, you are beyond the point of having only to give additional clarification and must deal with taking corrective action.

Generally, by the time you hear about a problem volunteer or have to deal with the individual, the staff or other volunteers already know about the issue. Everyone is waiting to see what you will do. In other words, you cannot ignore the situation and hope the problem goes away or that the volunteer will resign. You will seldom be this lucky.

Whatever steps you decide to take, it is important that your actions are covered within the volunteer handbook. This is easily accomplished with several statements that include the following points:

The use of volunteers is subject to the changing needs of the library.

Volunteers are responsible for following the library rules and policies as specified in the volunteer handbook.

Volunteers are subject to corrective action that may include being de-volunteered.

All volunteers serve at the discretion of the library director.

As the volunteer manager, you are the representative of the library director for the volunteer department. The statements above give you flexibility to take corrective actions when necessary, and to let a volunteer go if he or she is not working out or filling the needs of the library organization.

A volunteer handbook that clearly sets forth a set of workplace rules goes a long way toward avoiding future disciplinary actions.

Volunteer Corrective Action

Fortunately, there are few "problem" volunteers. Most individuals who want to volunteer at the library are supportive of the policies and conscientious about following instructions and rules. Problem volunteers usually have personality traits that are extremely difficult, if not impossible, to change. It is a good idea to set up corrective action procedures and summarize these in your volunteer handbook. Key ideas to keep in mind are:

Counseling versus corrective action;

Listening and fact finding;

Progressive corrective actions; and

Documenting actions.

COUNSELING VERSUS CORRECTIVE ACTION

A key reason why people volunteer their time and energy to serve the community is for personal reward and satisfaction. A volunteer seldom causes problems in task performance. Usually the individual has difficulty following or understanding a library policy or rule. You can get the volunteer back on track by showing empathy, and helping the individual understand what behaviors need to change and why. This process is defined as counseling. You are working through a problem with an individual to achieve a positive behavioral change.

Corrective action is taken when a volunteer chooses not to follow the rules and continues on the same negative path after counseling. This situation can result in the disruption of departmental procedures. At this point you need to take stronger measures to rectify the problem.

LISTENING AND FACT FINDING

One of your first responses to a problem situation should be to verify the information. This requires a combination of active listening and objective fact finding to gain insights into the real problem and to show that you are open to differing opinions.

If you find the problem is with a volunteer and your advice and counsel are not followed, then you want to issue a verbal warning and provide additional clarification of the rules. Most likely, the volunteer is not familiar with library protocol and is not clear about supervisory expectations. Be sure that you stay open to the volunteer's expressed concerns when you talk to him or her. You need to recognize that the first comments in the discussion are usually less important than what is said later in the conversation. For example, if a volunteer feels that the staff does not like her, you can ask the following questions to clarify the problem: "Who do you think doesn't want you to volunteer at the library? Why do you think they feel this way?" The initial response might be "everyone" or "all the staff." If you pause and do not answer her immediately, she will probably expand on her answer. If you find this approach difficult, you can ask a follow-up question to elicit a more specific answer: "Can you give me an example of why you think no one wants you to volunteer at the library?" You might find that only one staff member made a negative comment, or a comment was taken out of context. The volunteer generalized it to everyone's feelings about her and her work. In this situation, you can offer to talk to the staff member to see if additional training might help her improve her skills, reassign the volunteer to another job, or change her hours so that she is working with different people.

PROGRESSIVE CORRECTIVE ACTION

Progressive corrective action is going from a verbal to a written warning, then to forced leave of absence, and finally moving to de-volunteering. Unless your library policy requires you to follow these steps, you are not required to take progressive action against a volunteer. In fact, you might want to state in your handbook that if any corrective action is necessary, it can result in de-volunteering on the first offense. For example, one of your teenage volunteers is suspected of coming to work under the influence of illegal substances, or is caught taking money out of a cash register. In this case, you would de-volunteer the individual on the first offense. Fortunately extreme cases such as these seldom occur in a library. However, if such a situation does occur, you want to be prepared to send the volunteer home immediately.

When corrective action is necessary, you need a statement from the volunteer about the incident. A report is generated from her remarks and your own investigation. This is presented to the library director or senior administrator to determine what action the library wants to take. You need to be specific and document everything that is said or every action that occurred. In the case of attempted theft, you need to find out if a report with the police must be filed and if the library will prosecute the teenager. These decisions are usually made at a senior administrative level.

A volunteer who continually violates a minor safety rule may be subject to progressive corrective action. For example, a volunteer who is assigned to water the plants in the library is found using a swivel chair to reach a hanging basket in the reference area. You ask her to use the stepladder in the storage closet but she chooses to use the chair. This is an accident waiting to happen and exposes the library to an unnecessary safety risk. In this situation, you should use progressive corrective action. If this does not work, you are justified in removing her from the task. If you place her in another assignment that requires her to follow an established safety rule and she refuses, you can initiate de-volunteering.

Other situations where progressive corrective action might apply are violating dress codes, smoking, taking unexcused absences, taking library supplies, violating customer confidentially rules, having conflicts with staff, being rude to customers, and misusing the telephone or fax machine.

DOCUMENTING ACTIONS

During a busy day, it is hard to recall who said what and when, especially when there is a potential for conflict. It is a good idea to make written notes when you take an action that you feel might have broad ramifications for the library. One option is to keep a notebook and jot down what you did and the date. You can also write a note in your computer notebook or in the volunteer's file. In most situations, your notes are memory cues to help you act with consistency. If you tell a volunteer she can change her days during the week, your note is to remind yourself to tell the supervisor of the change in hours.

In the case of a problem volunteer, your notes serve as documentation of your conversations and decisions. Often problem volunteers have a way of changing interpretations as they recall meetings or conversations. Your notes are written for your eyes only and help you clear up any confusion. In the case of de-volunteering, they become the documentation that leads to this decision. However, you need to be aware that these notes can become matters of record in an administrative hearing in the library, or they may be used by a third-party agency if the volunteer takes legal action. You do not want to write something for the file that can reflect poorly on you or the library.

The most likely legal charge would be discriminatory conduct as seen from the volunteer's perspective. For example, a volunteer privately tells you she has tested positive for HIV, and four months later the supervising staff member wants her replaced because she has made numerous task errors that affect productivity. You have no other appropriate volunteer positions, so you have to de-volunteer the individual. A week later, you receive a letter from an attorney representing the local AIDS organization. It states that you discriminated against this individual by de-volunteering her after you learned she was infected with the AIDS virus. Suddenly your notes become part of an internal library review. Similar issues can occur with homosexual volunteers or any other individuals from a group viewed as a minority. Fairness and objectivity are important values to hold, especially during a corrective action process.

Corrective Action

Below are three sample dialogs that illustrate varying degrees of corrective action.

INFORMAL

Sally, you as a volunteer and I as a staff member both have to follow library guidelines. I know you did your best when you were told to straighten the newspaper shelves, but you threw out all the papers except last week's issues. The library's policy is to hold all newspapers for two months. If you do not know what to do, please ask for clarification from the reference staff or come to me. You can even give me a call at home. I know you pride yourself on being fast and efficient, but please do not let something like this happen again.

FORMAL

The rules and polices of the library are designed to support efficient operations to better serve our customers. As a volunteer your cooperation in following the rules will make your experiences rewarding. It is anticipated that you will not purposely violate established library policy and that any violation will likely result from not receiving adequate training. You are encouraged to ask questions if you do not understand something. Any consistent violation of library rules and guidelines will lead to a reassignment to more closely supervised volunteer duties or asking you to give up your volunteer position.

DISCIPLINARY

In order to serve our customers and the community and to meet agency requirements, the library has a set of expectations and rules that all staff and volunteers are expected to comply with while working at the library. Volunteers who violate posted or written rules will be subject to disciplinary action. Disciplinary action may include (1) joint discussions with the volunteer manager and library manager; (2) reassignment to a new set of volunteer duties; (3) an informal request for resignation; or (4) de-volunteering. Any volunteer can appeal a decision to the library director who will then review the circumstances and actions taken.

SECTION

33

De-volunteering

Most of the time, a verbal warning is enough to change the work behavior of a volunteer so that she or he is in sync with library expectations. You need to understand de-volunteering, however, because of the occasional problem volunteer. There is no requirement to keep someone because that person wants to volunteer in a library. If an individual is not working out after you've tried corrective action, then for the sake of the library organization, staff, customers, and other volunteers, you need to initiate the process of de-volunteering. When you do, it is important to keep the following points in mind:

Preliminary de-volunteering actions;

Setting the time and place;

De-volunteering conversation;

Reference request; and

Appeals process.

PRELIMINARY DE-VOLUNTEERING ACTIONS

Once a decision is made to dismiss a volunteer, the key reasons for de-volunteering are written down in notebook style. Also include a summary of specific policies or rules that were violated and where they appear in the volunteer handbook. If the issue is performance, get a copy of the volunteer job description or task list and check off which tasks were not performed to library standards. If the issue was a personality clash with a staff member, write down how you feel this conflict affected the department.

Second, write down the sequence of actions you took to improve or correct the situation (use any personal notes or calendar dates to help you recall the events leading up to the de-volunteering action).

A hypothetical example of a de-volunteering action is the case of a volunteer who was hired to shelve library videos. According to her supervisor, she was not putting the videos back in correct order. You and the supervisor meet to discuss the situation because several customers have complained about the lack of order in the video section. After discussing several options, the supervisor agrees to provide the volunteer with additional training before any action is taken. After several weeks, it becomes apparent that the situation does not improve. Customer complaints have increased. You hold a second meeting with the supervisor. At this time, you both agree to either dismiss the volunteer or find her a new job in another department.

The first step you take in this situation is to look at the job description. Under "duties," it states "accurate shelving of videos and other media according to the Dewey Decimal System." Because this volunteer's only problem was with "accurate shelving," you decide to give her another opportunity in the circulation department mending books. You meet with her and explain the situation by referring to the job description as a reason for changing her duties.

Throughout the sequences of events, you maintain an informal diary of dates, conversations, and actions taken to resolve the problem. If the volunteer works out performing basic mending and cleaning, the issue is resolved. However, if she is unhappy with the move and displays her displeasure through careless mistakes and verbal complaints overheard by others, you will have to consider de-volunteering. Review your notes with a library administrator to keep any decision objective. As a manager, you cannot ignore this situation.

There is more likelihood that you will have to de-volunteer one of the court-ordered "volunteers." Court-ordered individuals pose a slightly different problem because they often choose the library as an "easy place" to perform their community restitution services. They can show a limited desire to work at an acceptable level. When problems occur because of performance or absenteeism, you can immediately de-volunteer them if you feel it is necessary. In this situation, it may be useful to get a third-party opinion. Introducing a third party into the situation gives you a cooling-off period and a chance to gather and share your thoughts before you take action.

In circumstances that may involve a potential charge of discrimination, it is prudent to share your concerns with a senior personnel administrator or legal counsel before you initiate any de-volunteering action. The library policy in this area may be applicable to the procedures you use to de-volunteer. Once you decide to de-volunteer after a thorough examination of the facts, you can continue to set in motion the wheels to dismiss the volunteer.

SETTING THE TIME AND PLACE

For almost anyone, de-volunteering is a serious loss of face. It is difficult for most people to understand that they have been fired from their job. Therefore, to prevent unnecessary complications (such as lawsuits), it is a good idea to have someone else present, such as the immediate supervisor. Ideally, you want to meet the volunteer in your office or a place that is private. It is also important to talk to the volunteer before she or he starts work. The conversation should take no more than ten minutes, but block out fifteen to twenty minutes to make sure you write any pertinent notes while they are still fresh in your mind.

DE-VOLUNTEERING CONVERSATION

Keep in mind that this is an administrative decision based on objective facts. It is not a reflection on the volunteer as an individual, but rather on the individual in the role of a library volunteer. The objective basis for any de-volunteering action is in either job performance or violation of library rules.

Script what you need to cover in outline form. You are not required to, nor should you go into, detail about the basis for de-volunteering. Below is an example of a possible scenario, scripted to explain to June the reason why she is being de-volunteered:

> June, after four months with the library and three different assigned tasks, we made the decision that the library is not the best place for your volunteer efforts. We provided extra training, at your request, but your mending is still not meeting library standards. We appreciate your willingness to work with us in the library. I would be more than happy to help you find other volunteer work.

> Thank you for coming in today. I reserved the study room so that you and I can discuss your work as a volunteer. During the past two months, I have spoken to you about your rudeness to our customers. I also explained to you on two prior occasions how important our community residents are to the library. Last night you lost your temper and became rude to a family with small children. The manager telephoned the family and apologized on behalf of the library. You may recall that I offered you the position of book wrapper, a position that does not require customer contact. You said you were not interested in this position. My only recourse now is to remove you from the volunteer schedule. As of this afternoon, you are no longer a library volunteer. You are certainly encouraged to use library services as a community resident. I hope you will continue to do so and to support the library. There are other volunteer opportunities within the community and I trust you will find one that is more suited to you and your needs.

The volunteer may request a second chance or want to know specifically what she or he did wrong. Your answer must be brief and to the point: "It is your overall performance that is not meeting standards. This is not related to any particular event or day." You need to be firm but always polite; stay in control of the conversation. Even if the issue is a personality trait (e.g., aggressive, domineering, or confrontational) or a communication style (e.g., boisterous or abrasive), your answer stays the same: "you are not meeting library standards."

After a brief explanation, your goal is to bring the conversation to a polite end. At this time, stand up and move to the door to indicate an end to the conversation.

In preparing for the meeting, run through a checklist of any library-owned items the volunteer may have including keys, instructional manuals, borrowed equipment, and so forth. Be sure to arrange to get these items back.

REFERENCE REQUESTS

If the volunteer asks you to be a reference, you can base your decision on library policy. In some situations, you may agree to be a reference if you know this is a hardworking individual who had difficulty learning a library task. In other situations, you may want to only fill out a work verification form.

Individuals who need credit volunteering will probably want the hours they earned at the library. If you have a third-party agency form that you need to complete, decide whether or not to indicate that you de-volunteered the individual. How honest you want to be is probably going to depend on your library policy. If in doubt, get advice from the library director or legal counsel.

APPEALS PROCESS

If a volunteer feels that he or she was treated unfairly by you, the staff, or the supervisor, he or she must have the right to appeal a decision that affects his or her status as a volunteer. The appeals process must be part of your volunteer policy manual, as well as clearly outlined in the volunteer handbook.

The first step in the appeals process is a meeting with the immediate supervisor. The volunteer should bring a written memo (providing you with a copy) to the meeting outlining his or her grievance. This memo becomes part of the formal process. If the volunteer is not satisfied with the supervisor's response, he or she can present the case to you, the volunteer coordinator, then your supervisor, and finally the director of the library. After formal appeals fail, the volunteer can take his or her grievance to legal counsel. It is very important for you to keep a diary of the events and document everything. File your notes in a confidential folder, with copies of the pertinent information to your supervisor.

34

Exit Interviews and References

As you review your library volunteer program over a period of time, you will notice that some individuals work for a month, others for eight to ten months, and some for many years. Whether an individual voluntarily resigns or quits without notification, she or he has information about his or her volunteer experience that can be useful to you for improving your program. One way to capture these insights and experiences is through an exit interview or mail-in questionnaire. This needs to done as soon as you are aware that the volunteer is about to leave or has formally left the program. However, this procedure should not be followed in the case of forced resignations or de-volunteering.

Section 34 will discuss the following key points:

Exit interviews;

Exit mail surveys;

Data interpretation and reporting;

Separation forms; and

Letters of reference.

EXIT INTERVIEWS

An exit interview is a structured set of questions that a volunteer is asked at the time the volunteer is leaving or has already left the library (see sample 34-1). The interviews are given in person or over the telephone.

Volunteer Name_____ Date_____

As you look back over your library volunteer experience, do you feel your personal needs were met?

___ Yes, most of the time   ___ Seldom met

___ Yes, some of the time   ___ Not met

Comments _____

_____

Do you feel you received adequate training to perform your job(s)?

___ Yes   ___ No   ___ Not sure

Comments _____

_____

Do you think your staff supervisor was effective in making you feel part of the library team?

___ Yes   ___ No   ___ Not sure

*Explain*_____

_____

Would you encourage your friends to become library volunteers?

___ Yes   ___ No   ___ Not sure

Comments _____

_____

What can we do to make the library volunteer program better?

Comments _____

_____

Interviewer _____   Title _____

Creating Questions

You can learn about the quality of your program though questions on training and placement, the relationship between the volunteer and staff, supervisors, and other volunteers, the assigned work, suggestions for improving the program, and the reason(s) for leaving. Questions about the volunteer experience are based on their personal reflections, such as the opportunities that enhanced goals, the chances to learn new skills and meet people, job satisfaction, and recognition.

Initially, the process of researching and developing questions and learning to conduct an oral interview without biasing the results may take a disproportionate amount of your time. However, it will be worthwhile because it will give you in-depth knowledge of your program, the library, and volunteers. First, look at your program from all angles (recruitment, placement, supervision, job duties, and recognition) to decide on the type of data you want to collect so that you can develop the questions to reflect the information you need. This may take a minimum of a year working with the volunteer program. Finally, attend workshops or courses on interviewing techniques to learn how to conduct oral interviews without biasing the results.

EXIT MAIL SURVEYS

An alternative to personal interviews is the exit survey that can be mailed to former volunteers (see sample 34-2). Mailed questionnaires, however, are not always filled out and returned. You can increase your odds of receiving a response by including a personal cover letter explaining the purpose of the survey, and a stamped, addressed envelope marked "confidential."

An easy-to-use form can be designed so that the questions can be answered by a checkmark under a specific category such as "satisfied," "very satisfied," and so forth. This type of questionnaire, however, limits the scope of a response because the answers do not account for individual feelings or experiences. Therefore, to make sure you are getting the total picture, include space for written comments. The form should be easy to read and limited to a single page so that it takes five minutes or less to complete.

The mailed questionnaire should include the same questions as the formal exit interview so that you have a basis for comparing the answers between volunteers who leave abruptly without a word and those who acknowledge their departure. If you find similar answers, you know which areas are weak in your program.

SAMPLE 34-2
Volunteer Mail Survey

Please take a few minutes to answer several questions about the Volunteer Program at the _____ Library. Your comments are important and will help us improve our program in the future.

Thank you for your time.

Sincerely,

1. Were your personal needs met as a library volunteer? *(Check one)*

   ___ Yes, most of the time   ___ Seldom met

   ___ Yes, some of the time   ___ Not met

   Comments _____

   _____

2. In comparison with other volunteer experiences, how would you rate your volunteer time with the library? *(Check one)*

   ____ Better   ____ Worse than

   ____ Equal to   ____ I have had no other volunteer experience

   ____ Somewhat less positive

   (continued)

Comments _____
_____

3. Did the library give you adequate training to perform your job(s)?

___ Yes   ___ No   ___ Not sure

Comments _____
_____

4. What additional type of training would you have liked?

Comments _____
_____

5. How effective was your staff supervisor in helping you become part of the library team?

___ Highly effective   ___ Not very effective

___ Somewhat effective   ___ I never felt part of the team

6. Were you encouraged by the library supervisor to offer suggestions on ways to do your volunteer job better?

___ Yes, most of the time   ___ Not too often
___ Only at times   ___ Never encouraged to offer suggestions

7. Did you feel you received recognition for your efforts?

___ I was well recognized   ___ Rarely recognized

___ I received a few positive ___ Never recognized
     comments

8. Do you feel you were kept informed of changes in library policies and procedures that affected your volunteer work?

___ Yes, all the time   ___ Only on rare occasions
___ Yes, most of the time   ___ Never

9. Would you encourage your friends to become library volunteers?

___ Yes, definitely   ___ Maybe
___ Yes, with qualifications ___ Not sure

Comments _____
_____

10. How would you make the library volunteer program better?

Comments _____
_____

Name *(optional)*_____

Thank you. Please return this questionnaire in the stamped,
preaddressed envelope at your earliest convenience.

INTERPRETATION OF DATA

Whether you use an exit interview, a mailed questionnaire, or a combination of both, you need to know how to use the information you get to your best advantage.

If your question response categories are, for example, "highly enjoyable," "very enjoyable," "not enjoyable," and "definitely not enjoyable," you are eliminating a neutral category (no opinion), which forces the volunteer to choose between opposite experiences. Therefore, in interpreting the answers, you can combine all the "highly enjoyable" and "very enjoyable" responses and get a single total. Do the same for the negative experiences. Convert the respective totals into percentages by dividing them by all the exit interviews done over a three-month, six-month, or one-year period.

If 60 percent, 70 percent, or even 80 percent of your former volunteers check off positive comments, you can take credit for having a program that meshes well with the volunteers' requirements and experiences.

Negative experiences, on the other hand, provide you with information on changes that you might consider in the program. Usually these comments fall into general categories with specific complaints under each one. Serious comments need to be looked at immediately. These include complaints such as "nowhere to store personal effects," "inflexible scheduling," "poor treatment by staff," "lack of volunteer identification," or "little appreciation." First, however, you must verify the validity of the remarks and the extent of the problem if it concerns a department, branch, or staff member. One of the simplest approaches in this case is to discuss the complaints with a few of your respected volunteers. They may have experienced the same feelings or situations, thereby validating the complaints. They may also make positive suggestions to improve the situation.

Problems identified by complaints that indicate a lack of understanding or knowledge can be remedied more easily. For example, those complaints mentioned above that deal with recognition (i.e., "lack of identification" and "little appreciation") can be eliminated in the future by providing name badges or identification cards to all volunteers and encouraging staff to be more attentive to the volunteers and their work. Except for some focused time, neither of these actions is financially costly, yet both will go a long way toward giving personal recognition to your volunteers for work well done.

Finally, make sure you discuss the results of your questionnaire with your supervisor. Comments that seem unrelated may actually be part of a larger problem.

SEPARATION FORMS

In a small community library, the use of a separation form may be administrative overkill. Merely shifting a volunteer's application from the "active" to "separated" file and the addition of a final work date are all that is necessary. In larger programs, using a separation form is a way to organize information (see sample 34-3). This form can include:

Dates of volunteering;

Volunteer position;

Department or branch;

Staff supervisor;

Job effectiveness;

The reason for leaving; and

Return of any library equipment,
    keys, and so forth.

Separation forms are useful if you receive a call for a reference and need to quickly refresh your memory or know who to ask for information.

Volunteer Name_____ Volunteered from _____ to _____

Volunteer position(s) held _____

Volunteer staff supervisor_____ Department _____

Reason for leaving

Took paid employment

___ Another volunteer position   ___ Personal time for family

___ Personal travel   ___ Medical condition

Other _____

Has the volunteer returned all library keys, equipment, and materials?

___ Yes   ___ No

Did volunteer give notice?

___ Yes   ___ No

Explanation _____

Overall, how effective was the volunteer in performing duties for the library?

___ Very effective   ___ Not effective

___ Effective

Comments _____

_____

Signature _____ Date _____

Title _____

LETTERS OF REFERENCE

Depending on your library policy and your workload, you may want to offer to write a letter of reference for volunteers seeking employment or going to another organization.

In the cover letter that is sent with the questionnaire or at the end of the exit interview, you can indicate that you are willing to write a letter of reference based on their volunteer experience if one is requested by their future employer. This is a gesture that ends their time with you on a positive note.

There are two kinds of reference letters: (1) For the individual who was an average or below-average volunteer, you can write a "neutral" letter acknowledging that the individual worked for you. Be sure to include the dates that he or she volunteered and the tasks performed for the library. (2) For the exceptional volunteer, you can include the aforementioned information, amplifying specific areas of excellence and personal comments that demonstrate your knowledge of his or her work (see sample 34-4).

Date

Ms. Patty Adams
Community Volunteers Inc.
3333 West Sunnyvale Drive
American City, OK 99999

Dear Ms. Adams:

It is my pleasure to recommend Molly Jamison for the position of administrative assistant to your nonprofit group. I have known Molly as a volunteer in our library for over two years. During that time, she donated over two hundred hours. Molly was an enthusiastic volunteer. She started with us cleaning books in the Technical Services Department. Then she was trained to update the business reference loose-leaf service. This takes a detailed individual to correctly file and maintain the weekly reports. Our head reference librarian, who found it to be 100 percent accurate, recently reviewed her work. She is also skilled in word processing and several other database programs. In fact, several months ago I asked her to develop a volunteer database and was extremely pleased with the way this project turned out. She and I worked closely over a three-week period to get the data table formatted for useful reporting. She had the patience to make the numerous changes and enter the data accurately. Molly did an outstanding job. Recently her personal circumstances have changed so that she has to seek full-time employment.

Molly has excellent computer, office, and people skills, as well as an enthusiasm to tackle the most challenging problems. She will be missed around here.

I give Molly my strongest recommendation. I am sure she will be an outstanding employee for you because she was one of our best volunteers.

Please feel free to call me if you would like any additional information.

Sincerely,
Name
Title
Phone number

SECTION
35

Volunteer Personnel Files

A new volunteer manager may start out with an odd assortment of names and telephone numbers on scratch notes, files that are obsolete, or nothing at all. Organizing information on the active volunteers means setting up a minimum filing system that keeps track of these individuals. When starting or updating a record-keeping system, be sure to include the following key components in each volunteer file:

- Application forms;
- Volunteer agreements;
- Emergency contacts;
- References;
- Performance evaluations;
- Letters of reference;
- Separation forms; and
- Record retention policy.

APPLICATION FORMS

A volunteer application form is the most important document in your personnel file. This form contains all the relevant information about an individual applying for a volunteer position. Depending on how sophisticated your program is, you can have the following types of applications: (1) general community, (2) court-ordered, and (3) a shorter student form. Whether you keep separate files for each type of volunteer or combine them into a single file depends on the number of people volunteering in each category.

Not everyone who completes the application form becomes a library volunteer. You can keep the applications of individuals not selected for a few months in case the situation changes. Also, you can set up an active pending file of applicants who are willing and able to volunteer when the library has a suitable opening.

Whether you choose to have a single file folder (or large three-ring notebook) labeled "Active Volunteers" or separate folders for each individual depends on your available time, needs, and space limitations. Regardless of your decision, each completed form must be kept confidential. Where a person lives, works, or the reason why they are volunteering is no one's business but yours at this point.

If at all possible, have your own file cabinet or at least a file drawer with limited access. Be careful not to write interview notes on the application form. These should be kept in a separate location until the applicant is accepted as a volunteer, and then discarded.

VOLUNTEER AGREEMENTS

The second most important set of documents in your files is the signed volunteer agreement forms. You may use just one document that formally states the rules the applicant agrees to abide by in exchange for the opportunity to volunteer at the library. The form, once signed, serves as the basis of a mutual agreement as well as providing a reason for dc-volunteering a person whose actions violate the rules.

Consent agreements that allow you to get a personal background check from the police department, a current copy of a driving record, screening for drugs, and so forth are documents that should be kept in the volunteer personnel files. These signed forms become very important if information is discovered that prevents an individual from becoming a volunteer. She or he can register a formal complaint against you or the library, or threaten to take legal action.

EMERGENCY CONTACTS

Your application form may have an emergency contact number for a volunteer but in practice if the form is in your files and you are not around, the collected information becomes useless in the event of a medical emergency. One option is to have a separate, short form or card file that can be conveniently kept by the immediate supervisor. Then the emergency information is readily available if it is needed.

REFERENCES

Some volunteers will bring with them a letter of reference. It can be kept with the application form. However, when you do reference checks on potential volunteers, whether by telephone or via a standardized mailed form, you want to keep this information separate from the application. You may receive negative or confidential information that should not be part of the volunteer's personnel file. Your library administrative rules may state how long you can hold this information, but in general, once you make a decision, the letter of reference or any notes should be removed from the file.

For example, during a telephone reference check, you are told that an applicant had serious difficulties as a volunteer at a local school. The reference did not want to give you any details but suggested you check for yourself. When you call the school, the principal politely states that she cannot give references for either staff or volunteers according to school policy. However, she does verify that the person was a volunteer. At the moment you have unsubstantiated information about possible problems. Whatever you choose to do at this point should be based on library policy.

Your written notes need to stay in your own file and not become part of the volunteer's application file.

PERFORMANCE EVALUATIONS

Whether a supervising staff member writes a short note about a volunteer's performance or you complete a formal evaluation form, these items become part of a volunteer's file. Similarly, if a customer writes a complimentary letter about a volunteer, this also becomes part of that file.

In most cases, performance comments serve as useful feedback to the volunteer. Most people want to know how well they are doing and positive comments serve as personal rewards. These notes

act as reminders when you have volunteer recognition events and you want to say a few words about each volunteer.

When the comments are not positive, the forms serve to document a volunteer's performance when it was not up to library standards and what action was taken. In either instance, these evaluative forms and notes become part of the volunteer's formal record.

LETTERS OF REFERENCE

You may be asked to write a letter of reference for a volunteer seeking full-time employment. If you have had a long and close relationship, this is easy to do. In most cases, however, the volunteer may have worked in the library at odd times when you

were usually not around. This is when any evaluative notes, forms, or "letters to the file" are helpful for writing a good reference. Remember to put a copy of the letter in the volunteer's file so that you have a record of what you wrote and to whom you sent it.

SEPARATION FORMS

In a small volunteer program, you may have only a note saying that a volunteer is going to be doing something different and will no longer be volunteering after a specific date. In other cases, you may write a note that the volunteer has not come in or called for the past three weeks and you

assumed she quit. In a more formalized program, you may actually use a separation form indicating that a follow-up phone call was made, the dates of the person's volunteer activity, and why she or he is no longer volunteering.

RECORD RETENTION POLICY

How long should you retain your volunteer files? The easiest solution is to follow the retention policies of your human resources department (if you have one) dealing with staff files. If you do not have such a department, keep the applications for a minimum of six months, especially in the case of a volunteer who was rejected. This enables you to respond to any questions, negative comments, or legal issues that might arise. In an active pending file, after six months many people have gone on to other adventures and you may want to make a follow-up call to see if they are still interested in volunteering.

For people who have volunteered for any length of time, you may want to hold their files for one year in the event the individual wants you to verify volunteer time for a third party (e.g., an employer). Unless you have an excellent memory, you may not recall each volunteer and what he or she did. Unlike the records of paid staff, library volunteer records are not subject to wage and hour reviews or IRS inquiries, so there is no legal need for maintaining the information. You may want to review your record retention plans with a library administrator.

36

Volunteer Administration Records

The accumulation of materials on managing a successful volunteer program can be overwhelming. For this reason, you want to identify which records, forms, and information you need to do your job effectively. If you set up general administrative files at the beginning, it is easier to organize your efforts as your volunteer program expands.

By organizing your files according to the following categories, you can access the necessary information quickly and efficiently:

Time and attendance records;

Job descriptions;

Departmental request forms;

Recruitment sources;

Skill inventories;

Quarterly/annual reports;

Forms; and

General volunteer information.

TIME AND ATTENDANCE RECORDS

Whether you use daily, weekly, or monthly volunteer sign-in sheets or keep individual time cards, you need to keep these time and attendance files for data-reporting purposes. This information is used to reward volunteers based on their number of donated hours and to report to the administration actual community involvement. It also serves to indirectly demonstrate the success and value of your program.

Accessing the collected data from a software program will streamline your operations and enable you to produce various reports depending on the information you need at the time.

JOB DESCRIPTIONS

Your files contain forms that document the volunteer positions. These may be formal job descriptions, task cards, or task lists that you can share with potential volunteers. You can keep these in a three-ring notebook or in separate files, depending on how many kinds of positions you have available.

DEPARTMENT REQUEST FORMS

In a formal program, you can design a form that is used by supervisors to request volunteers with specific skills. These completed forms become the basis for recruitment campaigns to fill the requested positions. In less formal programs, your file may contain notes or memos from staff requesting volunteers with specific skills and/or time requirements. This file is the counterpart to your "Active Pending Volunteer File" and, ideally, you will have a volunteer in the pending file that can be matched with your request form for specific kinds of volunteers. Keeping your request forms organized makes it easier for you to remember the types of volunteers you currently need; however, the matching process is not always so simple. A library manager may want someone to clean books on Monday and Wednesday mornings when there is a staff member available to supervise, but none of your active pending volunteers have that time slot available. Now you need to reevaluate your available volunteer pool to see who is available to meet the departmental request. One way to set up your files so that this information is always at your fingertips is to use a volunteer tracking sheet (see sample 36-1).

RECRUITMENT SOURCES

One useful file to develop is a list of contacts that you can depend on to give you information about sources for potential volunteers. This file can be transferred to a database or Rolodex files. Any system you choose should be convenient and easy to use.

Also include successful examples of flyers, posters, announcements, and other recruitment ideas, as well as the locations for posting. There is very little that is totally new or different, so use your creative ability to blend examples to come up with unique recruitment approaches that work for you.

SKILL INVENTORIES

Whether you use checklists of interest areas or formalized skill inventories, you need to know the skills and interests of your volunteers to match individuals with available positions. This type of information lends itself well to a database that can quickly match a volunteer's skills and interests with a job. It is this kind of "perfect" match that makes the volunteer manager's job so fulfilling.

SAMPLE 36-1
Volunteer Tracking Sheet

NAME   PHONE

STREET   CITY   ZIP

Approximate age: _____ Facility preference: _____

Birthday (month/day) _____

Days/hours preferred per week: _____

Position/area desired: _____

Special skills mentioned: _____

_____

Application mailed: _____ Returned: _____ Name tag ordered: _____
              DATE   DATE   DATE

Contacts, notes, and action taken:

QUARTERLY/ANNUAL REPORTS

Your administrative files will contain statistical reports either on a monthly, quarterly, or annual basis. These reports should contain the number of volunteers, their donated hours, projects, and any other information useful to you or your administration. See examples of a monthly volunteer report (sample 36-2) and a cumulative volunteer report (sample 36-3).

This is also a good place to put informal notes about particularly successful volunteer projects and events that you want to call attention to in your next report. Trying to summarize a year's worth of work from memory is difficult. If you learn to put "memory reminders" in your file, it will help to make the end of the year reporting process easier.

FORMS

Inventory your volunteer program forms (applications, agreements, time records, releases, etc.) and estimate how many you will need over the course of six months. Building a small inventory will save you time in the future.

February ____

Volunteer Categories

Branch/Department	Community Volunteer		Friends of the Library		School Volunteer		Civic/Social Org. Vol.		Court-Ordered Worker	
	Persons	Hrs.	Persons	Hrs.	Persons	Hrs.	Persons	Hrs.	Persons	Hrs.
Philip S. Miller	10	52					2	17	10	124
Parker	6	40	3	26	1	18			13	126
Highlands Ranch / Rox.	8	56			3	10			10	83
Lone Tree	1	10	1	12	1	8			7	118
Louviers										
Tech. Services										
Adult Literary Program	16	210								
Adm./Programming	2	11							1	2
Local History	5	114								
Books-by-Mail	3	13								
District Totals	51	506	4	38	5	36	2	17	41	453

District Monthly Summary

	Persons	%	Hours	%
Community, Friends, School, Civic Volunteers	62	60%	597	57%
Court-Ordered Workers	41	40%	453	43%

Compiled by _____

SAMPLE 36-3
Cumulative Volunteer Report

Volunteer Categories — Second Quarter 2001

Branch/ Department	Community Volunteer		Friends of the Library		School Volunteer		Civic/Social Org. Vol.		Court-Ordered Worker	
	Mo/Avg Persons	Hrs YTD	Mo/Avg Persons	Hrs YTD	Mo/Avg Persons	Hrs YTD	Mo/Avg Persons	Hrs YTD	Mo/Avg Persons	Hrs YTD
Philip S. Miller										
Parker										
Highlands Ranch / Rox.										
Lone Tree										
Louviers										
Tech. Services										
Adult Literacy Program										
Adm./Programming										
Local History										
Books-by-Mail										
District Totals										

District Second Quarter Summary

	Mthly Avg Persons	Type of Vol %	Total Hours YTD	Type of Vol %	Monetary value to DPLD YTD
Community, Friends, School, Civic Volunteers					Hours * $7.50/hr
Court-Ordered Workers					Hours * $5.15/hr

Compiled by _____

159

GENERAL VOLUNTEER INFORMATION

There is a growing body of volunteer literature including general articles, books, and Internet sites. Some of this material is pertinent to library volunteer programs. One way to keep your enthusiasm growing and bring innovation to your program is by reading current materials. For example, a hospital may use an idea to attract volunteers that you may like to try, a copy of a form used by a local museum can be modified to serve your needs, or an idea for a guest speaker is found in a local newspaper article. These ideas cover the whole realm of volunteerism and come from many sources. By drawing on others' ideas and experiences, you can develop your own individual volunteer resource file(s).

BIBLIOGRAPHY

Volunteers in Libraries

Beauregard, Sue-Ellen. *Volunteers: We Couldn't Do without Them!* Chicago: ALA/Library Video Network, 1998. (Video)

Boatner, Debra K. "Volunteers: The Hope for Tomorrow's Library." Master's thesis, George Fox College, 1992.

Bolt, Nancy. "How to Have a Successful Volunteer Program." *Colorado Libraries* 17, no. 2 (June 1991): 7-8.

"Book Buddies Deliver to Homebound" (program for older adults at the Lexington Public Library; reprinted from page 1, November/December 1995). *Unabashed Librarian,* no. 98 (1996): 6.

Brown, Candice. "Public Library Service to the Homebound." *Colorado Libraries* 16, no. 3 (September 1, 1990): 14-15.

Chadbourne, Robert. "Volunteers in the Library: Both Sides Must Give in Order to Get." *Wilson Library Bulletin* (June 1993): 26-27.

Childs, Catherine C. "Cunning Passages, Contrived Corridors: Mobilizing Volunteers for a Public Library Tour." *Public Libraries* 32, no. 3 (May 1, 1993): 143-146.

Childs, Catherine C., and John Waite Bowers. "Introducing the Colorado Libraries Volunteer Managers Council." *Colorado Libraries* 23 (summer 1997): 36-39.

Conway, P. S. "Examining the Basics: Work, Jobs and Income (Economic Impact of the Volunteer Labor Market)." *Public Library Journal* 15, no. 1 (spring 2000), 17-18.

Driggers, P. F. "Risk Management for Volunteer Programs." *Colorado Libraries* 26, no. 1 (spring 2000), 45-46.

Hedges, Cheri and Stephanie Span. "Good Volunteer Management Helps Make the Difference." *Ohio Libraries* 4 (July/August 1991): 20.

Heiserman, Jo Ann. "Library Directors and Volunteer Programs." *Colorado Libraries* 17, no. 2 (June 1991): 16-17

Jervis, B. "Unpaid Volunteers: Burden or Bonus? (in Public Libraries in Great Britain; Survey Results)." *Public Library Journal* 15, no. 1 (spring 2000): 15-16.

Johnston, Ray. "Helping Hands: Volunteers Build a New Library (Pilomath, Oregon)." *Wilson Library Bulletin* (January 1994): 25.

Karp, Rashelle. *Volunteers in Libraries.* Small Libraries Publications, no. 20. Chicago: ALA, 1993.

Manning, Mary. "Public Library Volunteers: Ya Gotta Love 'Em . . . or Do You." *Public Libraries* 35 (November/December 1996): 336-372.

McCune, Bonnie F. "Marketing to Find Volunteers." *Colorado Libraries* 26, no. 3 (fall 2000): 40-41.

———. "The New Volunteerism: Making It Pay Off for Your Library." *American Libraries* 24, no. 9 (October 1993): 822-824.

McCune, Bonnie F. and Charleszine Nelson. *Recruiting and Managing Volunteers in Libraries: A How-to-Do It Manual.* New York: Neal-Schuman, 1995.

McGrath, Marsha. "Teen Volunteers in the Library." *Public Libraries* 29, no.1 (January 1, 1990): 24-29.

Nicely, Connie. "Rural Library Volunteers." *Colorado Libraries* 17, no. 2 (June 1, 1991): 11.

Reed, Sally Gardner. *Library Volunteers Worth the Effort! A Program Manager's Guide.* Jefferson, N.C.: McFarland, 1994.

Ross, Janet. "Success with Volunteers." *Library Mosaics* 6, no. 4 (July 1, 1995):19.

Schmidt, David. "Wanted: Library Volunteers." *Colorado Libraries* 20, no. 1 (spring 1994): 15.

"Self-service at Montgomery City; If Budget Gets Cut, Branches May Be Staffed Primarily by Volunteers." *Library Journal* 117 (April 1, 1992): 24.

Sherman, G. W. "How One Library Solved the Overcrowded Storytime Problem (Marshall Public Library Uses Volunteers)." *School Library Journal* 44, no. 11 (November 1998), 36-38.

Smith, Marsha Anderson. "The Library Volunteer Program in Recessionary Times: An Interview with Bernie Margolis and Debbra Buerkle at Pikes Peak Library District." *Colorado Libraries* 17, no. 2 (June 1991): 9-10.

Wakefield, Barbara. "Court Ordered Volunteers." *Colorado Libraries* 17, no. 2 (June 1991): 18.

"Ways to Recognize Volunteer Service." *Unabashed Librarian,* no. 113 (1999): 17.

Wells, L. B. "Volunteers in the Libraries." In *The Library Trustee.* 5th ed. Chicago: ALA, 1995, 172-180.

White, Herbert S. "The Double- Edged Sword of Library Volunteerism." *Library Journal* 118 (April 15, 1993): 66-67.

General Works on Volunteerism

Allen, Ken. *Creating More Effective Volunteer Involvement.* Washington, D.C.: Points of Light Foundation, 1996.

American Association of Retired Persons. *Bringing Lifetimes of Experience: A Guide for Involving Older Volunteers.* Washington, D.C., 1994.

Campbell, Katherine Noyce and Susan Ellis. *The (Help!) I Don't Have Enough Time Guide to Volunteer Management.* Philadelphia: Energize, 1995.

Ellis, Susan. *Focus on Volunteering Kopy Kit.* 2nd ed. Philadelphia: Energize/Parlay International, 1998.

———. *From the Top Down; the Executive Role in Volunteer Program Success.* Rev. ed. Philadelphia: Energize, 1996.

———. *The Volunteer Recruitment Book.* Philadelphia: Energize, 1994.

Ellis, Susan and Katherine H. Noyes. *No Excuses: The Team Approach to Volunteer Management.* Philadelphia: Energize, 1981.

———. *Proof Positive; Developing Significant Volunteer Recordkeeping Systems.* Philidelphia: Energize, 1990.

Fischer, Lucy Rose and Kay Banister. *Older Volunteers; a Guide to Research and Practice.* Thousand Oaks, Calif.: Sage, 1993.

Graff, Linda. *Beyond Police Checks: The Definitive Employee and Volunteer Screening Guidebook.* Dundas, Ont.: Graff and Associates, 1999.

———. *By Definition: Policies for Volunteer Programs.* Philadelphia: Energize, 1993.

———. *By Definition: Policies for Volunteer Programs.* 2nd ed. Etobicoke, Ont.: Volunteer Ontario, 1997.

Harrington, Walt. "Volunteers; How Helping Others Helps You Change Your World." *Washington Post Magazine* (December 19, 1993): 10-15+.

Lee, Jarene Frances, Julia M. Catagnus, Susan J. Ellis, eds. *What We Learned (the Hard Way) about Supervising Volunteers.* Collective Wisdom Series. Philadephia: Energize, 1998.

Logan, Suzanne. *The Kids Can Help Book.* New York: Putnam, 1992.

Lynch, Rick and Sue Vineyard. *Secrets of Leadership.* Downers Grove, Ill.: Heritage Arts, 1991.

McCurley, Steve and Rick Lynch. "Supervising the Silent Volunteer." *Grapevine,* May/June, 1995.

———. *Volunteer Management: Mobilizing All the Resources of the Community.* Downers Grove, Ill.: Heritage Arts, 1996.

McCurley, Steve and Sue Vineyard. *101 Ideas for Volunteer Programs.* Brainstorm Series. Downers Grove, Ill.: Heritage Arts, 1986.

———. *101 More Ideas for Volunteer Programs.* Brainstorm Series. Downers Grove, Ill.: Heritage Arts, 1995.

McKaughan, Molly. *Corporate Volunteerism: How Families Make a Difference.* New York: The Conference Board, 1997.

Minnesota Department of Human Services. *Measuring the Difference Volunteers Make: A Guide to Outcome Evaluation for Volunteer Program Managers.* Ed. Melissa Eystad. St. Paul: Minnesota Department of Human Services, 1997.

Minnesota Office of Citizenship and Volunteer Services. *Playing It Safe: How to Control Liability and Risk in Volunteer Programs.* Rev. ed. St. Paul: Minnesota Office of Citizenship and Volunteers, 1998.

Minnesota Office on Volunteer Services. *Playing It Safe: How to Control Liability and Risk in Volunteer Programs.* St. Paul: Minnesota Office of Volunteer Services, 1992.

Pidgeon, Walter P. *The Universal Benefits of Volunteering.* Somerset, N.J.: John Wiley, 1997.

Points of Light Foundation, Nonprofit Risk Management Center, and the American Bar Association. *No Surprises Controlling Risks in Volunteer Programs.* Washington, D.C.: 1993.

Scheier, Ivan. *Building Staff/Volunteer Relations; a Positive Approach to a Universal Challenge.* Philadelphia: Energize, 1993.

Stallings, Betty. *Resources Kit for Managers of Volunteers.* Pleasanton, Calif.: Building Better Skills, 1992.

———. *Training Busy Staff to Succeed with Volunteers.* Pleasanton, Calif.: Building Better Skills, 1996.

Sutton, Charyn D. *Pass It On; Outreach to Minority Communities.* Philadelphia: Energize, 1992.

Tremper, Charles and Gwynne Kostin. *No Surprises: Controlling Risks in Volunteer Programs.* Philadelphia: Energize, 1993.

Vineyard, Sue. *Beyond Banquets, Plaques and Pins.* Downers Grove, Ill.: Heritage Arts, 1982.

———. *Evaluating Volunteers, Programs and Events and Reflection: The Evaluative Component of Service-Learning.* Downers Grove, Ill.: Heritage Arts, 1994.

———. *Finding Your Way through the Maze of Volunteer Management.* Downers Grove, Ill.: Heritage Arts, 1982.

———. *Marketing Magic for Volunteer Programs.* Downers Grove, Ill.: Heritage Arts, 1984.

———. *New Competencies for Volunteer Administrators, Self-Study Guide.* Washington, D.C.: Points of Light Institute, 1998.

———. *Secrets of Motivation: How to Get and Keep Volunteers and Staff.* Downers Grove, Ill.: Heritage Arts, 1991.

Wilson, Marlene. *The Effective Management of Volunteer Programs.* Boulder, Colo.: Volunteer Management Associates, 1976.

———. *You Can Make a Difference.* Boulder, Colo.: Volunteer Management Associates, 1990.

Associations

Association for Volunteer Administration (AVA). AVA, P.O. Box 32092, Richmond, VA 23294.

Newsletters

DOVIA (Directors of Volunteers in Associations). Over 360 groups located throughout the United States.

Grapevine. CAHHS, Volunteer Sales Center, P.O. Box 2038, Sacramento, CA 95812-2038.

Points of Light Foundation, 1400 I Street, NW, Suite 800, Washington, DC 20005 info@pointsoflight.org

INDEX

volunteers
    definitions of, 56
    legal definitions of, 23-24

W
waivers and releases, 81-83
    samples, 82-83
Web pages, 58-59
welcome letter, 91, 92
wellness manual, 103-104

women as volunteers, 53
work space for volunteers, 16, 22
Workers' Compensation, 28-29
written communications, 32, 34

Y
young adults
    application forms, 61
    definition of, 56
    and job skills, 6

    as volunteers, 25-26, 53
    waivers and releases, 81-83
Youth at Risk programs, 26
youth volunteers, definition of, 56.
    See also Young adults

Preston Driggers is the Personnel and Risk Manager for the Douglas Public Library District in Colorado, and has worked in both private and public human resources management for more than twenty-five years. Driggers is an active participant in the Colorado Libraries Volunteer Managers Council. He is an associate faculty member of Regis University, where he teaches courses in organizational behavior, human resources, and the sociology of work. He is also actively involved in efforts to preserve open space land.

Eileen Dumas is a special services librarian at the Aurora Public Library in Denver and has worked in volunteer management since 1991. She is actively involved in local volunteer organizations, including the Adams/Arapahoe Retired Senior Volunteer Program, Metro Libraries Volunteer Management Council, and Denver DOVIA. From 1998 to 2000, she edited a column, "Volunteer Line," that appears in the spring and fall issues of *Colorado Libraries*. In 2002 Dumas became co-editor of this journal.